SUE BECKER'S HOMEMADE BREAD, SOUPS & STEWS COOKBOOK

SUE BECKER'S HOMEMADE BREAD, SOUPS & STEWS COOKBOOK

Family Recipes Made with Home-Ground Flour and Wholesome Ingredients

Robert Rose

To my husband, Brad, and all of my family and friends who have shared and enjoyed a bowl of soup and warm bread with me over the years. You are greatly loved and appreciated.

For complete cataloguing information, see page 288.

Design and Production: PageWave Graphics Inc.
Editors: Jennifer MacKenzie and Kathleen Fraser
Indexer: Gillian Watts
Cover and Food Photography: Natercia Cabeceiras
Food Styling: Sonia Lizotte
Author Photo (page 9): Tiffany Thompson
Additional Photographs (page 12, 23, 25, 31): © Getty Images
Illustrations: © Getty Images

Published by Robert Rose Inc.
120 Eglinton Avenue East, Suite 800, Toronto, Ontario, Canada M4P 1E2
Tel: (416) 322-6552 Fax: (416) 322-6936
www.robertrose.ca

Printed and bound in China

1 2 3 4 5 6 7 8 9 ESP 34 33 32 31 30 29 28 27 26

CONTENTS

Preface

Family Recipes for Homemade Bread, Soups and Stews

When I think about my family recipes, I think of comfort foods, foods made at home with love. Comfort foods can satisfy your hunger but they can also warm your heart with pleasant memories of special people, places and events in your life.

For me, one such comfort food is, of course, bread, but to that I'd add tomato soup. Just the thought of tomato soups stirs up sentimental emotions and memories of my younger self being served Campbell's tomato soup from a can with a grilled cheese sandwich, especially when I was sick in bed.

Today, I enjoy making delicious soups and bread from scratch. To me, there is nothing quite as comforting as baking bread made from home-ground flour and preparing homemade soup with wholesome, everyday ingredients, and then sharing them with family. The aromas that fill my kitchen when I'm cooking are an invitation for all to come and enjoy.

In this book, you will find recipes for many types of soups, stews, chilis and, of course, breads that have become some of our family favorites over the years.

All of my bread recipes are made with freshly milled flour, because that is who I am and what I am all about. To get you started (if you haven't already discovered the joy of home-ground flour), I've included some general instructions on milling your own grains, the best home flour mills, and some basic how-tos of bread making with freshly milled flour. I've included a variety of yeast breads and quick breads, and all the information you need to know to make them nutritious and delicious.

Over many years of cooking, baking and preparing food for our large and busy family, I have discovered the incredible time-saving benefits of using pressure cookers, especially for soups, stews and chilis.

Of course, you don't need a pressure cooker to enjoy the great recipes in this book: each recipe includes both regular stovetop instructions and pressure cooker instructions, with a few exceptions where a pressure cooker isn't practical.

For each soup, stew and chili recipe, I have also recommended my favorite bread to accompany that particular dish.

I think there is nothing better than a bowl of hot soup or hearty stew served with fresh warm bread to give the comfort and nourishment we need to face whatever life brings our way. It is my pleasure to share with you some of my favorite recipes, with the hope that, whether through the abundant nutrition in each homemade bite or the fond memories they invoke, these breads, soups and stews will become some of your family's favorite comfort foods.

About Sue

I was born and raised in Savannah, a coastal town in the state of Georgia in the southeastern United States. Growing up in the 1950s was vastly different than it is today. We rarely went out to eat. Meals were home-cooked from scratch, and "supper," as we call it in the south, was the evening meal when we all sat down together.

I grew up loving to learn to cook. Like most kids, I loved helping my mom in the kitchen and I still remember her words as she taught me how to scramble eggs. I loved choosing recipes from cookbooks and accepting the challenge to make them.

My teen years came with many extracurricular activities, leaving me little time to cook at home, but home economics courses in middle school and high school greatly sharpened my cooking skills. While I thoroughly enjoyed these classes, a new course of study caught my interest. Science!

I loved biology, physiology and microbiology. I studied everything about the human body and how it worked. It was only natural that after high school I would head off to college, to the University of Georgia, as a premed student. I had a passion to help people get well and, in my mind, I wanted to save the world.

It didn't take me long, however, to realize that a medical career was not for me. So I landed in food science, an up-and-coming industry at the time. After graduation, I worked nearly five years as a bacteriologist for a major food company.

Yet my passion for studying the human body and the way it works never waned. I loved a good biochemistry book and studying the scientific works of those in medical and healthcare fields.

I believed then, and now, in healthy eating, and eating real food. After the birth of my first child, I quit my job and became more committed than ever to a healthy lifestyle. My husband, Brad, and I had a huge garden. I prepared most of our food from scratch. Mealtime was real meat, real homegrown vegetables, real butter, real fruit and even homemade bread. Much like the meals I grew up enjoying.

But to be honest, neither I nor my family loved the bread. I was making it with commercially processed whole wheat flour, but it was dry, coarse and crumbly. I gave up on making bread with 100 percent whole wheat flour but still made from scratch our muffins, pancakes, pizza dough and dinner rolls, adding a bit of whole wheat to the white flour, hoping that would improve the nutritional value.

Other than our bread, our diet was pretty well built on real food, much of it from our own garden. And for the most part, our family was fairly healthy. Our kids, however, still had their fair share of colds and ear infections and seemed to catch whatever bug was going around. I personally had the common complaints of many Americans — constipation, chronic sinus congestion, frequent headaches, even migraines occasionally. I was also tired all the time. By the time we had five children, I was blaming my low energy on being a wife, nursing mother and homeschooling mom.

But in 1991, my world changed when I was introduced to the concept of milling whole grains to make my own flour at home.

I knew from my years of study that whole grains are among the most nutrient-dense food groups and they provide many of the vital nutrients and fiber that promote good health. Digging deeper, I learned that only when grains are freshly milled do they retain all of these life-giving nutrients.

Real whole-grain flour spoils and, to prevent spoilage, mills were invented to remove the bran and germ portions of the grain, as well as the oils within those components. However, with this removal, most of the nutrients are lost. After the invention of the steel rolling mills in the late 1800s, and the introduction of long-lasting white flour and white bread in the early 1900s, and as this bread and flour became the food of choice, there appeared to be a related decline in the health of Americans.

Today many common health complaints in America can be traced to the missing nutrients that are no longer provided by commercially processed bread, even when it is said to be enriched. As I continued to study, even going back to my food science text books, I learned that this enrichment replaces a mere fraction of the nutrients lost when the bran and germ portions are removed from the flour.

More than ever, I became convinced that freshly milled whole-grain flour was the way to go. And surprised that with my background in food science and all my studies, I had not put all these pieces of the puzzle together before. Relating many common health ailments to commercially processed flour products seemed a very broad statement, but my personal experiences and continued study were soon to prove it persuasive.

I was ready to put this information about whole-grain flour to the test when the idea of milling my flour at home became reality. My enthusiasm for what I had learned led Brad to buy me my first grain mill, a small electric mill made for home use, for my birthday in February 1991. That mill, bought more than 35 years ago, was definitely the start of something big!

From the day the mill arrived, I began making all of my own flour at home for all our bread, muffins, pancakes, biscuits, cakes, and cookies — anything made from flour for my young family. I was convinced that white flour would never be a part of my bread making again, and decided that I would be making only what I call "real bread" with 100 percent freshly milled whole-grain flour.

Starting that very first day, after eating the most delicious bread I had ever made, I already noticed significant health benefits. In the first 24 hours, my lifelong struggle with constipation was ended, never to return. Within a few days, I noticed increased energy. I no longer needed

or even wanted a nap just to function. By the end of the first month, my frequent headaches were gone, chronic sinus congestion, gone, and my daily dependence on antihistamines, gone!

And none of these chronic issues have returned in all these 35-plus years of real bread. I've not had an antihistamine of any kind since 1991. My children's frequent colds and other sicknesses became almost non-existent. And in 25 years of raising now nine children, only three doctor visits were needed for our children.

I could hardly believe the vast difference this one change in our already healthy diet seem to make in the health of our family. I needed to know how and why. Thus began my journey of in-depth study of the many nutrients supplied by whole grains and freshly milled flour and the role they play in meeting the physical needs of our bodies. I read everything I could get my hands on. And what I read confirmed that whole grains are indeed one of the most nutrient-dense food groups God has given us.

In my excitement I began to share my bread with others. Very soon, they were calling me, wanting more bread. They shared with me how they too had more energy, were no longer struggling with bowel issues or just simply felt better since eating this real bread.

The next thing I knew, I was making and selling bread out of my home and tiny kitchen. But with the birth of my sixth child, I was quickly becoming overwhelmed.

One day, in the fall of 1992, after a long day of making bread for others, making bread for my family, homeschooling the children and taking care of my family's needs, I realized that making bread for others was not the best plan.

That day, when Brad arrived home from work, I met him in the driveway to present my new idea: "I do not think I am supposed to make bread for the world but I am to teach the world to make bread for themselves." I believe that God put this idea and these words into my heart and mind, an inspiration that would change our lives forever.

Bread Beckers was born that day in 1992, on the driveway of our small home where we have raised nine children together. Our business grew from the testimonials of others and my teaching. By 1998, the business had outgrown our home and family, so we incorporated with a long-time friend and partner and moved into our current location in Woodstock, Georgia, in 1999. Today we occupy about 23,000 square feet of space between two buildings. We have a 10,000 square foot retail space with a studio classroom where we offer in person and online classes. We are now a large grain packaging facility servicing more than 150 co-ops throughout the country.

My passion to teach others how to make bread from freshly milled flour and the amazing health benefits of whole grains has never waned. In fact, I may be more passionate today than when I first started this journey 35-plus years ago. But over the years my message remains the same. God intended bread to be the staff of life. Jesus compared himself to bread for a reason — because real bread made from freshly milled whole grains is life giving and life sustaining. It is too good not to share with others.

Over these past 35 years, I have seen countless lives changed for the better. It is my continued passion to not only teach the world to make bread for themselves but also to come back to eating and preparing real food, and to share with others the skills I have learned over these many years of cooking, baking and preparing nourishing meals for my family. Enjoy!

"I knew from my years of study that whole grains are among the most nutrient-dense food groups and they provide many of the vital nutrients and fiber that promote good health."

Introduction

Baking with Freshly Milled Flour: Grains and Other Ingredients

While this cookbook is not an exhaustive guide to milling your own grains and making your own bread, all of the baking recipes (and some of the soups and stews), included here use only freshly milled flour.

You might ask yourself, Why should I make bread using only freshly milled flour? Here are a few of my favorite reasons.

Nutrition

Whole grains are unbeatable for their nutrient and fiber density. A nearly perfect food, whole grains supply all but a few of the essential nutrients our bodies need for health and wellness. But only when they are freshly milled just before baking do they retain all of these vital nutrients.

Delicious

Homemade bread, especially when made with freshly milled flour, is not only nutritious but also very delicious. It is full of flavor, unlike the tasteless commercially processed bread products offered to us in the store that are often artificially flavored and heavily sweetened.

Variety

We have a multitude of choices when it comes to using different grains and the unique flavor and texture profiles they offer to baked goods. When we can choose which flour we use, we open up a whole world of creative options. Simply changing the kind of flour we use in a recipe can result in a very different flavor or texture. For example, using freshly milled corn flour instead of soft wheat in a waffle recipe, as in the Corn and Jalapeño Jack Cheese Waffles (page 72), can take them from breakfast waffle to savory dinner waffle.

Before we get into the actual baking techniques of both yeast-leavened breads and quick breads, let's review some of the grains you can use to make your flour and their best application. Following are a few of the grains I have used in my baking. Feel free to incorporate other favorites in these recipes and elsewhere. As a great friend and chef once reminded me, "recipes are just suggestions." So be creative and make each your own.

If you want to read more about milling and baking techniques and find more recipes for bread, biscuits, cookies and cakes, you may want to pick up a copy of my best-selling *The Essential Home-Ground Flour Book, Second Edition* (Robert Rose, 2026).

Which Grain to Use and When

All About Wheat

Wheat is the world's most important grain crop. It ranks first among grains for its nutritional value and baking qualities. Since the beginning of time, wheat has reigned king for bread baking.

When used in its entirety, wheat is an excellent source of fiber and many critical nutrients. The germ of the wheat kernel is one of the richest food sources of Vitamin E, and the bran supplies many minerals, vitamins and phytonutrients that are lost when these components are removed. Milling your own flour at home allows you to enjoy bread that supplies these nutrients because the bran and germ remain in the flour.

Wheat is important not only for its nutritional value but also its baking qualities. Wheat contains two specific proteins that are unique to the wheat family of grains. When wheat flour is fully hydrated, these two proteins, gliadin and glutenin, form a stretchy substance called gluten. In yeast-leavened breads, it is these stretchy strands of protein that enable bread to rise by trapping the CO_2 gas produced by the yeast organisms during the fermentation process of the dough.

Wheat is the only family of grains that contains these two unique proteins, making it superior for baking. The wheat family includes such grains as common bread wheat, spelt, Kamut (also called Khorasan) wheat, durum wheat, rye, and the ancient grains einkorn and emmer.

Common bread wheat is the most widely grown type of wheat. It is able to adapt to either winter or spring planting, and in diverse climates with varying rainfall, giving rise to thousands of varieties, each suited to the growing conditions of the region. The amount of rainfall during the growing season has given rise to two basic classifications of common bread wheat — hard wheat and soft wheat. These terms refer to the physical characteristics of the grain itself and are often used to determine what wheat is best for the desired baking application.

Hard wheat is grown in colder and dryer climates with little rainfall during the growing season, producing a grain that is high in protein. The protein content in hard wheat is generally between 12 and 14 percent. This high gluten-forming protein content is important for use in yeast-leavened breads, including sourdough, as these proteins develop the strong elastic strands that will stretch and allow the bread to rise. Hard wheat is preferred for yeast-leavened breads.

Soft wheat is typically grown in regions with higher rainfall during the growing season or with irrigation. It is characterized by softer, plumper kernels that are more easily crushed or chewed. It is lower in protein, with less tendency to form strong gluten strands. Often referred to as pastry wheat, it is the preferred choice for cakes, cookies, biscuits and pie dough, and can be used in yeast-leavened breads that don't require much rise, such as pita or focaccia.

Within the classes of wheat are two strains — red and white wheat, both available as hard and soft. The names generally refer to the color of the wheat but the main difference is flavor.

Red wheat has more tannins in the bran, giving it a darker, red color and contributing to the stronger flavor of the flour.

White wheat has less tannins, so is therefore lighter in color and milder in flavor than red wheat.

While I typically love the rich flavor of hard red wheat in my yeast breads, I prefer to use hard white wheat for pizza

crust or yeast breads that are filled with herbs and spices, when I want these flavors and not the flavor of the wheat to be dominant. But most often I use a combination of the two, usually two parts red wheat to one part white wheat. The same is true for soft red wheat and soft white wheat. While the flavor of soft red wheat might be great in a plain biscuit or waffle, I prefer the mild flavor of soft white wheat in the Dill and Feta Cheese Drop Biscuit or the Peppery Cheese Bread, so the flavors of the seasonings and cheese are not overpowered.

Part of the beauty of milling your own grain is that there are so many options and flavor profiles to choose from, instead of being stuck with the blandness of commercially processed white flour. And that leads me to share other grain flour options used in the recipes in this book. The first few are in the wheat family.

Other Grains

Most of these grains can be used in your favorite recipes, as long as you consider the right grain for the type of recipe you are using and the different density if measuring using metric weights (see chart page 24). Some flours made from grains other than regular wheat absorb liquid differently (the hydration quality), so I've added variations and tips throughout the recipes in this book on how to change the grains and get good results. It may take some trial and error to get the substitutions right, but I encourage you to try.

Spelt is one of my favorite ancient grains, with a flavor more like red wheat. I call it the wheat of both worlds. It mills up light and airy like soft wheat, so is great for making quick breads such as muffins, pancakes, cakes and cookies. But it also has enough protein to develop fairly nice gluten structure for making delicious yeast breads as well. You will typically require more flour in a recipe when substituting spelt for hard wheat.

Kamut® is the brand name for Khorasan wheat. It is the king of pasta-making but also delightful in muffins or pancakes. It is best in yeast breads when mixed with hard wheat. In fact, my favorite yeast bread combination is Kamut and red wheat, usually in a 1:2 ratio.

Rye, a close relative of wheat, is a little trickier to work with and, when making yeast bread, is best mixed with a hard wheat. While it does have a unique flavor, the distinctive flavor most associated with rye is caraway seeds, not rye flour itself. So don't be afraid to use some rye flour in your muffins and pancakes too.

Oats are a soft grain that is wonderful in quick breads and cookies. Oat groats are used to mill into flour, while rolled oats (also known as oatmeal) are made by passing the soft oat groats between two rollers to flatten them into flakes. Rolled oats may be added to yeast breads or quick breads to lend a nice texture and flavor. It is important to note that rolled oats cannot be milled into flour using an impact mill or burr (stone) mill. You must use raw oat groats.

Corn. White or yellow, dent corn or popcorn, all have their place in home flour milling. As with red and white wheat, the difference between white and yellow corn is mostly in flavor. Dent corn is a larger kernel so will yield a softer texture flour when milled in most electric mills, especially the impact mills. Popcorn will yield a coarser flour, perfect for creating a texture more like cornmeal. For most of my cornbread recipes I use whatever corn I have on hand.

Other Ingredients

Sweeteners

Raw honey is my preferred sweetener. A general rule of thumb is the darker the honey, the stronger the flavor. A mild honey will be lighter in color and add the least flavor to your bread.

Unrefined cane sugars can be used as alternatives for conventional white sugar and brown sugar. I use honey granules as my standard sweetener in place of granulated sugar. This is a granular product made from cane sugar with a mild-flavored honey added. Honey granules are available at specialty stores and online. You can use an equal volume or weight of other light-colored, fine-textured granulated cane sugar in these recipes. Dark unrefined cane sugar, such as Sucanat®, is my preferred brown sugar ingredient and can be used in equal volume or weight in recipes.

Dark unsulfured molasses is a by-product of the refining process of table sugar. Blackstrap molasses is rich in nutrients including vitamin B_6, potassium, calcium and iron. It adds a bold, rich flavor to breads.

Pure maple syrup. Unlike the cheap imitation maple-flavored syrups lining grocery shelves, pure maple syrup comes from the sap of the sugar maple trees. It is made by boiling the sap until enough water is evaporated to form a thick syrup. I don't often use it in baking but it can be used as a 1:1 substitute by volume for honey in most recipes. Its mild flavor is perfect for adding a little sweetness to some soups.

Fats and Oils

Extra virgin olive oil is my oil of choice. Other oils may be used, but this is the oil I choose for my family. Look for a reliable source, bottled in the country of origin.

Unsalted butter is what I use in all of my recipes. I want to control the amount and kind of salt in my food. Butter imparts a definite softness to the texture of bread, so it may be used in place of oil in most any recipe.

Coconut oil may be used in most any recipe for oil or butter in an equal volume or weight if a dairy-free option is desired.

Eggs add flavor, color and strength as well as nutrients to breads. Eggs are naturally high in fat and lecithin, so they contribute a soft, smooth texture to the dough and finished bread. Large-size eggs are the standard for baking recipes.

Lecithin is a fat emulsifier. I like using it in my yeast breads, as it gives the bread a soft crumb and smooth texture. It also helps the bread hold its texture during storing. It is an optional ingredient. You can make great bread without it, but you can make really great soft bread by adding it. My preference is sunflower seed lecithin powder.

Leavening Agents

Yeast is a living organism used as the leavening agent in yeast breads. During the fermentation process it produces CO_2 gas, which is trapped by the elastic strands of gluten, allowing the bread to rise. The recipes here call for quick-rising (also called instant) yeast. When using quick-rising (instant) yeast, you do not need to dissolve it in water. It can be added right along with the flour. You can substitute active dry yeast in these recipes, though it's best to dissolve the yeast according to package directions before mixing in the dry ingredients. Yeast likes a warm, humid environment. Liquid temperatures are important. If too hot, the yeast will die and the bread will not rise. If too cold, it will still rise but very slowly. About 110°F (43°C) is the optimal liquid temperature for the recipes in this book. The strain of yeast used for baking, *S. cerevisiae*, is very different from the problematic *Candida* strain of yeast.

Sourdough starter is a symbiotic culture of *Lactobacillus* organisms and various strains of yeast each working together. With the popularity of sourdough breads today, you can easily obtain a sourdough starter from an enthusiast who will be more than happy to share some with you. Or you can make your own. I have given detailed instructions in my *Essential Home-Ground Flour Book, Second Edition*. When making sourdough bread, it is important to remember to feed your starter with enough flour and water to make active starter to use in a recipe and some to reserve as your mother starter, at least 6 to 8 hours before you plan to make the recipe.

Baking powder is the common leavening agent in non–yeast-leavened quick breads, and my preference is a non-aluminum product. It is incorporated into the flour along with the other dry ingredients. It is then activated, first when the liquids are added to the flour mixture and further by the heat during baking.

Baking soda is another common leavening agent used in quick breads. It reacts with acid ingredients such as buttermilk to produce CO_2 gas.

Equipment and Tools

Equipment Needed

Whether or not you are new to home flour milling, you may want to review my recommendations for choosing equipment and some basic instructions on how to use these tools.

A Grain Mill

First and foremost, you will need a grain mill. A dedicated flour mill makes milling your own grain into flour easier than you might think. The one you choose will depend largely on your needs and goals, your budget, the size of your family and whether this is a hobby or a lifestyle.

A micronizing mill, also known as an electric impact mill, uses stainless steel milling heads. It is by far the fastest and easiest to use, especially for beginners. If you have a large family like mine, or will be making a lot of bread at a time, you will find this kind of mill your best option. The milling heads are self-cleaning and very durable and most have a limited lifetime warranty. A micronizing mill will grind any kind of dry grain or bean into flour in a matter of seconds with the push of a button and is small enough to sit on the counter of most kitchens. Simply turn the mill on, pour the grain into the hopper, and the flour is captured in a closed container. No mess, no fuss — fast and easy, producing a pound of flour (454 g) in about 45 seconds. These are typically the least costly of the electric mills.

An electric burr mill consists of two grooved grinding plates (burrs), one of which stays stationary while the other rotates to grind the grain in between. Today these milling heads are most commonly made of a composite material instead of stone. Most are encased in a beautiful wood housing that sit nicely on a kitchen counter with the flour flowing into an open bowl under the spout. They are considerably slower than the micronizing mills, taking 5 to 7 minutes to grind 1 lb (454 g) of flour, but will produce a wider variation of coarseness to fineness — from cracked grain, to coarse grind, to fine flour. Most electric burr mills cost considerably more than the micronizing mills.

A high-speed electric blender could be a great starter option if you already own one. But know that these will not produce near the quantity and fineness of flour as a dedicated mill. Buying one specifically to make flour might not be your best decision. Only small quantities of grain can be milled at one time. A blender may be a great "try to before you buy" option, but know that the flour is typically more coarse than what you can get from a dedicated grain mill. Coarser flour may mean heavier bread. This could turn you and your family off to the whole idea of using freshly milled flour, and we don't want that!

A hand grain mill is a great backup mill for a time when electricity might not be unavailable. It is a labor of love for anyone hoping to make bread made from freshly milled flour as part of a daily, healthy lifestyle routine. Usually a good hand mill will cost more than an electric mill. They are certainly versatile, with interchangeable heads that can mill not only grains and beans into flour but also nuts into nut butter.

A grain mill attachment to your stand mixer may be a good choice for some grain milling applications but most do not produce fine flour. These are my least favorite option. They are very slow and, on inferior-quality mixers, can cause wear and tear on the motor and transmission.

I am all for versatile, multi-use kitchen appliances, but a dedicated electric grain mill is the most valuable appliance on my kitchen counter.

A Stand Mixer or Bread Machine

You can make very good yeast breads by kneading the dough by hand. But a good mixer or bread machine will do a great job of kneading the dough, typically requiring less flour than hand kneading, and producing a less dense bread with a softer texture.

For most of my yeast-leavened bread recipes, I use a powerful, large-capacity stand mixer or even a bread machine to do my kneading. For any of the breads in this book, unless otherwise specified in the recipe, you can use the same steps when mixing and kneading by hand or using a stand mixer.

Other Tools and Supplies

Measuring cups (both nesting-style dry measures and liquid measuring cups with a spout and handle), measuring spoons, a good kitchen scale, a rolling pin, a pastry blender, bread pans, muffin pans and baking sheets may already be a part of your baking kitchen. If not, I recommend you invest in these tools.

Quick breads that don't use yeast as a leavening agent don't require any special equipment for mixing other than a good wire whisk and a mixing bowl.

For many of my yeast breads, I suggest using a baking stone or ceramic bread cloche (or a Dutch oven or cast-iron pot with a lid). If you do have any of these, don't be afraid to use them —the finished results are remarkable. If you don't have them, you might be adding them to your baking wish list soon.

Bread-Making Techniques: Yeast Breads and Quick Breads

Yeast Breads

Yeast breads are breads that use yeast as the leavening agent. They typically require both a kneading process and rising time.

Kneading the dough is necessary to "develop" the stretchy strands of protein, known as gluten. Gluten development gives yeast bread dough its structure and ability to rise. When kneaded sufficiently, the dough will look smooth and shiny and will be very elastic.

During the rising process, the yeast organisms feed on the carbohydrates in the dough, producing CO_2 gas as a by-product. The CO_2 gas is trapped in the elastic strands of the gluten. The gluten stretches and expands as it fills with the CO_2, enabling the dough to rise.

Some yeast breads, such as the Crusty No-Knead Bread on page 48, depend on time and hydration of the flour for gluten development. Because of that, they do not require kneading.

Basics of Yeast Dough Preparation

For most bread doughs that use oil or other fat, kneading the dough is an essential step to gluten development. It also incorporates and homogenizes the other ingredients into the dough.

A dough made with freshly milled flour will appear wet and sticky at first, but will gradually become smoother, elastic and less sticky as it is kneaded. It is important to note that freshly milled whole-grain flour is "thirsty," so it is okay to let the dough be wetter during this process. The fiber in the flour will continue to absorb moisture as it is kneaded, rests and rises. Do not be tempted to add more flour.

It is also important to note that unlike commercially processed white flour, which gives consistent baking results, freshly milled flour will vary from crop to crop, farm to farm and year to year. Hard red wheat grown in Montana may be very different from hard red wheat grown in Texas, Kansas or Canada. There is a bit of a learning curve, but you will get to know your dough and what it should look and feel like as you continue on this journey.

So, don't give up if you follow my recipes to a T and don't get the results you were hoping for. Recipes are mostly suggestions and a good starting point. Get to know the feel of the dough and make adjustments accordingly.

There are several techniques to making yeast bread doughs. Some people prefer to start with the dry ingredients and add the liquids. But because I find it easier to adjust the amount of flour needed than to adjust the liquids, I start with the liquid ingredients then add the flour as needed.

Steps for Bread Making in a Stand Mixer or by Hand

1. Combine the liquids. Yeast likes warm, not hot. I start with 110°F (43°C) water heated in my kettle. But you may use warm-to-the-touch water. I don't typically worry too much about this. Adding your other liquid ingredients, such as oil and honey, will cool the mixture a bit.
2. Add the salt and lecithin, if using, to the liquids.
3. Add part of the flour. Begin stirring the flour (using the dough hook of a stand mixer or a heavy-duty spatula or dough whisk by hand) into the liquids. Sprinkle the yeast over the top and continue mixing.
4. Add the rest of the flour gradually as specified in the recipes, as needed, until a soft dough forms and begins to pull away from the sides of the bowl. Knead in a stand mixer or by hand until the dough is elastic and looks shiny and smooth. This time will vary depending on the type of grain used for flour and the method for kneading.

Kneading Options

Kneading with a Spiral-Type Mixer Using a Roller Mechanism

Follow the steps above for preparing the dough. Once the first addition of flour and yeast are in the bowl, adjust the kneading arm as needed to prevent dough from pushing up and out of the bowl. Begin adding the remaining flour gradually, pulling the kneading arm toward the center briefly after each addition. With each pull of the arm to the center, watch for the dough to pull away from the sides of the bowl. When it does pull away, you have added enough flour. Knead for 5 to 10 minutes, depending on the amount of dough, until the dough is elastic and looks shiny and smooth.

Kneading with a Bread Machine

Almost any yeast bread dough can be kneaded in a bread machine and removed to shape as desired, allowed to rise and bake in your home oven. Simply add all of the ingredients called for in the recipe except the flour and yeast to the bread machine pan. Add the minimum amount of flour called for in the recipe. Make a slight indention in the center of the flour. Add the yeast into the indention. Put the pan in the bread machine and choose a dough-only cycle. When making a recipe for the first time in a bread machine, you might want to check the consistency of the dough after about 3 minutes of kneading, adding a little more flour if necessary. Once the kneading cycle ends, allow to rise in the machine or remove to an oiled bowl to let rise. Then, shape and bake as directed in the recipe. *As with any appliance, always read and follow the manufacturer's directions and, if the instructions differ from mine, adapt the recipes in this book for your bread machine as necessary.*

Kneading by Hand

After the initial addition of flour and yeast, you can either keep the dough in a large shallow bowl or turn it out onto a on a well-floured surface, then begin to knead the dough by flattening the dough with the heel of your hand, pushing down and away from you to stretch the dough (this helps the gluten form and stretch). Rotate the dough a quarter turn and fold the dough in half toward you. Push down and away with the heel of your hand. Rotate the dough another quarter turn and repeat the folding and pushing steps until a smooth ball of dough is formed. As you knead, you can add just enough flour to allow you to handle the dough but avoid making it stiff and dry. Let rise as directed in the recipe.

Rising

Bulk Rising

I usually like to allow my dough to bulk rise (also called proof) at least once. This is the first rise as outlined in my recipes. But this step can be very forgiving, as shorter or longer rises can be done. The rising time needed will also depend on the temperature and humidity (a warmer and more humid place will speed up the rise). When risen, the dough will typically look light and airy and double in bulk (size). Some recipes differ on the desired rising texture, so do check the instructions. You can let the dough rise right in the bowl of your mixer or the pan of your bread machine. Or you can transfer the dough to an oiled bowl. Cover the bowl.

Once the dough is doubled in bulk, you can punch it down to rise again (if the recipe instructs, for convenience or for a deeper flavor) or shape into your loaves or rolls.

Rising After Shaping

This is the critical rising time. Once your loaves or rolls are shaped, you should begin preheating your oven.

You will allow loaves to rise or proof until double in size or rolls until they appear light and airy. It is important that they go into the preheated oven to bake once they have risen sufficiently.

If the shaped loaves or rolls are over-risen or over-proofed, they will collapse while baking. Again, rising times will vary depending on the temperature and humidity of the environment. The warmer and more humid the room temperature, the faster they will rise.

I try to set a timer once my loaves are shaped (15 to 20 minutes is a good starting point). I will check on the progress and add more time if needed. Bake immediately when risen enough.

Quick Breads

Quick bread refers to breads that use baking powder and or baking soda as the leavening agents instead of yeast. They are exactly as their name implies — quick and easy to prepare.

Steps for Quick Bread Preparation

1. In a mixing bowl, whisk together all the dry ingredients called for in a recipe, such as flour, baking powder, baking soda, salt and any dry herbs, spices or sweeteners. Make a well in the center of the ingredients by whisking them away from the center of the bowl.

2. Add all the liquids into the center of the bowl. Stir with a whisk, spatula or spoon just until all dry ingredients are thoroughly combined. Do not stir until all liquids are added.

3. If doubling or tripling (or more) a quick bread recipe, I will combine the liquid ingredients in a separate bowl before adding them to the dry ingredients.

4. Bake as directed.

For quick breads such as biscuits or pie dough, you will cut the cold butter into the flour, using a pastry blender or two knives, before adding the liquids. Remember, freshly milled flour is warm, so for biscuits or pie dough you will want to chill your flour before cutting in the cold butter.

Weight Versus Volume

It has become increasingly popular in North America in the past few years to weigh ingredients for baking instead of measuring by volume. I will be the first to admit it is much easier to convert a processed flour recipe to freshly milled if the original recipe is written in weights. You simply use the same weight as called for in the recipe. You should get fairly consistent results.

But I have been cooking and baking for more than 60 years. I learned to cook and bake with standard liquid and dry measuring cups and I measure by volume. The recipes in this book were all developed using volume measurements. To accommodate those who prefer baking by weight, I have added metric weight measurements to all the recipes.

Most of us were taught that the correct way to measure flour by volume is to lightly spoon the flour into a dry measuring cup, then level off the excess by scraping a knife across the top of the measuring cup. Over the years, I have found that freshly milled flour is very aerated, so I can simply scoop up the freshly milled flour with a dry measuring cup, slightly shake the cup, then scrape with a knife to level. I have used this same measuring technique for all dry ingredients in this book.

The metric weights of ingredients in these recipes were calculated using my measuring technique. Rest assured that every attempt has been made to be as accurate as possible to give you the best finished result. But it is important to remember that even the same type of grain, and therefore flour, can vary in weight and moisture level from one season to the next and depending on where the grain is grown. You may need to adjust the amount of flour and/or liquid as you prepare each recipe.

It's always advisable to use only one method of measuring for a recipe: if you're measuring by volume, use the left-hand column in the ingredients list, and if measuring by weight, use the right-hand column. For very small amounts, like spices and leavening agents, it's fine to use the measuring spoon measurements in the volume column if your scale doesn't measure such small amounts accurately.

Metric Weight Conversions for Grains and Flour

Freshly milled flour is very aerated, so to achieve the conversions here, simply scoop up the freshly milled flour with a dry measuring cup, slightly shake the cup, then scrape with a knife to level.

GRAIN OR LEGUME	METRIC WEIGHT OF 1 CUP WHOLE GRAIN / LEGUME	METRIC WEIGHT OF 1 CUP FRESHLY GROUND FLOUR
Barley (hulled)	180 g	100 g
Bean (white, chickpeas / garbanzo beans)	200 g	115 g
Dried yellow or white corn (dent corn) or popcorn	220 g	140 g* (coarsely ground: 175 g)
Kamut	210 g	150 g
Hard wheat (red and white)	220 g	145 g
Rye	210 g	135 g
Soft wheat (red and white)	215 g	125 g
Spelt	200 g	130 g

*Dried yellow corn can be ground into flour or cornmeal; the weight of both grinds are the same. Coarsely ground corn, like that used for grits, has a greater weight per cup.

HOW PRECISE SHOULD YOUR MEASUREMENTS BE?

For Breads: Very Precise

The metric weights have been calculated as precise conversions from imperial volumes and should be followed to ensure good results with the recipe.

For Soups, Stews and Chilis: Fairly Precise

The metric weights have been calculated as precise conversions from imperial volumes. For ease, you can round the quantities up or down slightly and still get good results.

What Is the Yield of Flour from Grain Once It's Been Milled?

Ounce for ounce, pound for pound, gram for gram — the yield will be the same. So, 1 lb (454 g) of grain will give you 1 lb (454 g) of flour.

The weight will not change. Not so with volume measurements. When you mill your grain into flour, the volume will increase.

Over all the years of milling, I have found that most grains after milling, especially hard wheat, yield about half again as much flour as grain. For example, ⅔ cup of grain yields about 1 cup of flour and so on. It's not exact, but if you use this ratio, you will get pretty close to what you need for the recipe and it will keep you from milling too much. Higher-moisture grains such as soft wheat, spelt and rye will yield slightly more because they mill up a little fluffier than other hard grains. But I still use this basic conversion when determining how much grain to mill for the flour called for in a recipe.

The chart below is what I use to calculate how much grain I need to mill.

Grain-to-Flour Yield by Volume

CUPS OF GRAIN	CUPS OF FLOUR (APPROXIMATE)
⅓ cup	½ cup
⅔ cup	1 cup
1 cup	1½ cups
1⅓ cups	2 cups
1⅔ cups	2½ cups
2 cups	3 cups
2⅓ cups	3½ cups
2⅔ cups	4 cups
3 cups	4½ cups
3⅓ cups	5 cups

Soups, Stews and Chilis: Basics and Techniques

Looking for an affordable way to create a complete and healthy meal? The easy answer is soup, stew or chili. For the kind of comforting meal that just naturally invites you to sit down and enjoy, consider a warm bowl of goodness made with real ingredients, usually prepared with minimal fuss, in just one pot.

There are a great many soup, stew and chili recipes in this book to suit everyone's taste — and maybe to entice you to try something different. I invite you to dive in and try some of our family favorites — I have no doubt they will become yours as well.

The Wonderful World of Pressure Cooking

I was first introduced to the wonderful world of pressure cooking in the early 2000s. It was not a method of cooking I was familiar with growing up. But once I learned and experienced the ease, convenience and flavor that can be created in a short amount of time, I was hooked.

As a busy mom of a large family, and a business owner, getting healthy and delicious meals on the table as quickly as possible was game changer for me, especially when it came to hearty soups and stews. Using a pressure cooker cut the cooking time significantly, plus the flavor infused and retained in every dish was absolutely incredible. I was able to prepare full meals, including our favorite soups and stews, along with delicious hot bread, often in as little as 30 minutes.

While you can certainly prepare all of these soups and stews without a pressure cooker (and I have included conventional stovetop methods for each recipe), I am eager to introduce you to this wonderful world. I call it redefining fast food.

Why Use a Pressure Cooker?

Pressure cooking is a healthy and time-saving and flavorful way of cooking.

Healthy

Pressure cooking captures the nutrients in food, especially in those foods that need to be drained (such as vegetables). You can cook in less water than with conventional cooking, so fewer vitamins are lost down the drain. The shorter cooking times in pressure cooking also help to preserve some of the nutrients that can be destroyed by longer time exposure to heat.

Time Saving / Energy Saving

Cooking time for most foods, including soups and stews, is significantly reduced. Many foods need only one-quarter to one-third of the cooking time compared to conventional stovetop methods. For instance, whole-grain brown rice takes 1 hour to cook conventionally but only 18 to 20 minutes in a pressure cooker. Pressure cooking is energy-saving, as the shortened cooking times mean you use as much as 50 percent less energy. This can be a real bonus during the hot summer months, as shortened cooking times produce much less heat in the kitchen and home.

More Flavor

Cooking under pressure infuses flavor into the food. Foods cooked in a pressure cooker have a more intense flavor, and you will find you need less salt and seasonings.

Pressure cooking is a great all-season way of getting healthy meals, especially soups and stews, on the table in a short amount of time. My philosophy: Take the pressure of preparing meals off yourself and put it in the pot.

Pressure Cooker Basics

Today's pressure cookers are not like your great-grandmother's or even your grandmother's pressure cookers. Most are equipped with the following features, making them safe, quiet and simple to use.

- Heavy-duty and made from 18/10-gauge stainless steel
- An interlocking lid that cannot be opened until all the pressure is released
- A pressure indicator
- Automatic steam-release mechanism if the temperature and pressure in the pot increase too much

While I do prefer a stovetop pressure cooker for much of my cooking, electric cookers (often known as multicookers) are perfectly good for most soups and stews. They are virtually a "set and forget it" cooker for these hot meals. I hope that the following simple instructions for using a pressure cooker will make you feel more comfortable using either a stovetop pressure cooker or an electric one.

Steps to Cooking Under Pressure

Most modern stovetop pressure cookers have some sort of pressure indicator valve to show you what level of pressure, High or Low, has been reached. Pressure is measured in pounds per square inch (psi). High pressure is on average about 10 to 12 psi, while Low pressure is 5 to 6 psi. High pressure is ideal for cooking soups and stews. Electric pressure cookers allow you to select desired pressure setting and will automatically raise the cooker to pressure accordingly. Some electric pressure cookers have Low and High settings (sometimes Medium) that you select for cooking. I cook all of these recipes on High, but check your cooker's manual to see what pressure is recommended for different foods.

What follows are my general steps for pressure cooking. *Always read and follow the manufacturer's directions and if the instructions differ from mine, adapt the recipes in this book for your pressure cooker as necessary.*

1. Choose the right size pressure cooker for your recipe. You should always have a least 1 inch (2.5 cm) of liquid in the bottom of the pot but never fill the pot more than two-thirds full. Most pots have a maximum fill line, and the level of the food must not go above this line.

2. Prepare the recipe according to the instructions given, using the Sear or Sauté functions on an electric pressure cooker for the stovetop cooking steps where instructed.

3. Lock the pressure lid into place.

4. Bring up to pressure.

Stovetop pressure cooker: Over high heat, bring pressure up to High pressure on the pressure indicator, as outlined in the manufacturer's directions.

Electric pressure cooker: Set the pressure cook option and select the High or Low setting and manually set the cook time. Press Start.

5. For stovetop pressure cooking, reduce heat to maintain this pressure. (This is perhaps the most important step.)

Stovetop pressure cooker: This heat setting may vary from stove models, whether gas or electric. You will quickly learn the best setting on your stove to maintain this pressure. You want to avoid reducing the heat so much that the pressure level begins to drop. This will vary depending on how full the pot is. While you get to know your pressure cooker, keep a close eye on the gauge during cooking and be ready to adjust the heat as necessary until you get a better feel for how your cooker and stove work. Remember, it's never safe to leave any pot cooking on the stove without checking frequently.

Electric pressure cooker: Temperatures adjust automatically once desired pressure is reached. No manual adjustment needed.

6. Cook time starts once High pressure is reached.

7. When cooking is complete:

Stovetop pressure cooker: Remove pot from heat.

Electric pressure cooker: Turns off automatically when cook time is complete (you may need to press Cancel).

8. Let pressure release, using natural release or quick release:

Natural release for stovetop or electric pressure cookers: Let pot sit undisturbed until the pressure indicator valve drops completely.

Quick release for stovetop pressure cooker: Remove pot from the stove and, with lid remaining closed, set the pot in the sink. Run cold water over the edge of the closed lid until pressure indicator drops completely and all pressure is released.

Quick release for electric pressure cooker: Manually turn the valve on the top of the lid to Venting to release steam and pressure immediately

9. Open lid carefully: Even though the pressure has been properly released before opening, the contents in the pot are very hot and will release a lot of steam when the pot is opened, as any pot of hot food will. Remember to carefully open the lid away from you to avoid injury from the steam. Some foods need to be checked for doneness for food safety and/or tenderness, therefore they may need more cooking. In that case, return the pot to high heat and return to High pressure, then cook in short increments such as 2 minutes or 5 minutes at a time (to avoid overcooking) and release pressure as directed. Check the food again and repeat as necessary until the desired doneness is reached.

USING YOUR STOVETOP PRESSURE COOKER ON AN ELECTRIC STOVE

Gas stoves respond immediately to adjustment settings. Electric burners, on the other hand, take some time to cool down to the lower temperature. This often causes the pressure to continue to build above the High indicator while the burner is cooling. If the pressure goes beyond the High indicator, it will begin to release pressure out of the valve and around the lid. This safety feature prevents the pressure from building to dangerously high levels and is an indication that the burner setting needs to be lowered.

One trick I learned with electric stoves is to go ahead and reduce the heat when the pressure indicator reaches the Low-pressure indicator. The pressure will continue to climb to High while the burner takes its time to reduce the heat. Around the time the pressure has reached High, the heat of the element has reduced enough to keep the pressure steady. Alternatively, if the pressure gets too high, you can carefully slide the pressure cooker off of the burner and let the pot and the burner cool slightly, then return the pot to the burner.

Cooking Beans in a Pressure Cooker

Since learning to cook with a pressure cooker, I rarely buy canned beans or legumes to use in any of these recipes, especially since we sell dry beans in our business. Using a pressure cooker to cook beans makes it fast and easy to cook them ahead or while you are prepping the rest of the soup ingredients.

To Soak or Not to Soak

Most beans, with the exception of quick-cooking beans such as lentils or split peas, need to be soaked before cooking. For more even cooking and to eliminate water-soluble, gas-producing sugars, it is usually best to soak beans. Soaked beans will also take less time to cook.

When using a pressure cooker, there are two methods of soaking: the traditional overnight soak and the pressure cooker quick soak.

Traditional Overnight Soak

In a large bowl, completely cover beans with 2 to 3 inches (5 to 7.5 cm) of cool water. Let soak at room temperature from 4 to 8 hours, depending on the age and size of the bean. Older beans tend to dry out as they age and may take longer to soak up liquid. The larger the bean, the longer the soak. The beans will plump up and absorb much of the liquid. They've soaked long enough when you don't see them getting any bigger. Drain and discard soaking water and proceed with cooking as desired.

Pressure Cooker Quick Soak

In a pressure cooker, add beans and water in a ratio of 1:4 by volume (1 cup / approx. 200 g beans to 4 cups / 944 mL water), ensuring you don't fill the pot more than halfway. For each additional cup of beans being soaked, use a 1:2 ratio of beans to water. Add 1 teaspoon (6 g) of salt,

Smaller, more tender beans include adzuki, pinto, black and Great Northern or navy. Larger, firmer beans include kidney, fava or chickpeas (garbanzo beans).

if desired. Lock the pressure lid into place. Heat the pot over high heat and bring pressure to High. Cook for 2 minutes, adjusting heat to maintain pressure as necessary. Remove from heat and let pressure release naturally for 10 minutes. Quick-release the remaining pressure, if necessary. Drain and discard soaking water and and proceed with cooking as desired.

Pressure Cooking Soaked Beans

Place drained soaked beans in a pressure cooker and add enough water or stock to cover. Add ½ teaspoon (3 g) salt for every cup of beans. Lock the pressure lid into place. Heat the pot over high heat and bring pressure to High. Cook for 6 to 8 minutes for smaller, tender beans or 10 to 12 minutes for larger, firmer beans (see photo caption, page 29), adjusting heat to maintain pressure as necessary. Remove from heat. Let the pressure release naturally for best results.

TIPS

One cup (approx. 200 g) of dried beans yields about 2½ cups to 3 cups (425 to 510 g) cooked drained beans.

Choose the correct size pressure cooker for the amount of beans you are cooking. Beans and legumes bubble up significantly in a pressure cooker, so you must not fill the pressure cooker more than halfway.

For even cooking, be sure the beans are covered with water, stock or broth.

One 15-oz (425 g) can of beans yields about 1⅔ cups volume, including beans and liquid, and about 1½ cups (270 g) drained and rinsed beans, plus about ½ cup + 1 tbsp (155 g) liquid.

Stovetop Cooking

All the soup, stew and chili recipes included in this book may of course be cooked conventionally on your stovetop using a good heavy pot or Dutch oven.

I prefer to use a stock pot for soups, as they are tall and narrow, perfectly suited for making soups and stocks that use a large volume of liquid. Most come in sizes from 6 to 12 quarts (6 to 12 L) for home use. Stock pots typically have two handles (versus single-handled saucepans) to make it easier to lift a big, heavy pot of soup. For best results, to maintain a good simmer over low heat and to prevent scorching, especially of thicker soups and stews, you will want to choose a heavy-gauge stainless steel pot.

A Dutch oven–style pot, which is more wide than tall, is good for recipes that call for browning meat or sautéing vegetables before adding the liquids.

Either kind of pot is perfect for recipes that call for simmering for a designated time. Simmering is done over low heat, usually with the lid on to prevent evaporation of the liquids. Thicker soups may require more frequent stirring while simmering, especially near the end of cooking time. If a soup, stew or chili is getting too thick before it's finished simmering, simply stir in more stock, broth or water to thin to prevent it from sticking and scorching on the bottom of the pot.

Stock

The Essence of Soup Making

Chief among all the ingredients that go into soup is the stock, also commonly called broth, or bone broth in the case of poultry and meat versions. The flavor of most great soups depends on the flavor of the stock. For convenience, a good ready-made stock or broth can be a meal

saver, but homemade stock can be very simple to make and quite rewarding. For these recipes, I'm using the terms stock and broth interchangeably, and for the homemade recipes, I call them stock. Stock making does not need to be complicated or time consuming. A pressure cooker can make the process even faster. Stocks can be made in large batches and frozen for future use.

When choosing a ready-made stock or broth, I choose a good quality brand, the richer the flavor, the better. I typically do not choose a low-sodium or reduced-sodium broth, only because I don't care for the flavor. But you can always choose what works best for you and enhance the flavor with extra seasoning to your taste at the end of cooking.

There are no hard and fast rules for seasoning a stock. The recipes for chicken or turkey, beef and vegetable stocks on pages 88 to 92 are just suggestions with regards to the aromatics. You can vary the vegetables and spices to your taste and according to what you have on hand. I add salt when cooking stock, but you can leave it out and season with salt to taste when you use the stock.

One rule that does apply is to always start with cold water for stock making. Cold water draws out the flavors of the meat, bones and aromatics into the stock.

When making homemade stock, be sure to let the strained stock cool completely before storing. Large batches of stock, if not cooled before refrigerating or freezing, can actually warm up the freezer or refrigerator to an unsafe temperature. To cool stock quickly for optimal food safety, after straining, place the bowl or pot of stock into a sink full of ice water, refreshing ice as necessary, until stock is cold. I like to pour the cooled stock into glass jars, being sure to leave about $\frac{1}{2}$ inch (1 cm) head space if freezing.

Batch Cooking and Make-Ahead

Many soups, stews and chilis are even better the day after they are made, as the flavors have had more time to meld and intensify. Again, be sure to cool adequately using the ice-bath method as explained for stocks or by dividing into smaller containers to allow to cool at room temperature more quickly before freezing or refrigerating. Cooked foods should never be left in the food safety danger zone, 40 to 140°F (4 to 60°C), for more than two hours.

When reheating from frozen, you can let it thaw overnight in the refrigerator before heating or place the frozen soup in a heavy pot over low heat, breaking apart as it begins to thaw. Never thaw foods at room temperature.

Be sure to reheat until bubbling hot and heated through completely.

BREADS

YEAST BREADS

QUICK BREADS

Basic Yeast Bread

This is a great basic recipe for any bread baker and is my go-to dough for dinner rolls, buns, cinnamon rolls, doughnuts, pizza dough and more. Using only a few ingredients, the dough is easy to make and very forgiving even when too much or too little flour is added. This recipe uses no milk or butter and the egg is optional, as is the lecithin.

MAKES TWO 1-LB (500 G) LOAVES

- Two 8- by 4-inch (20 by 10 cm) loaf pans, greased or lined with parchment paper

Tips

You can make this dough in a 2-lb bread machine. Place the ingredients in the bread machine pan in the order listed. Set the machine on the dough cycle to shape and bake in the oven as directed or to use for one of the variations, or use the whole wheat cycle for a machine-baked loaf.

For a softer texture crumb and lighter loaf, you can substitute 1½ cups (360 g) warmed milk (approx. 110°F / 43°C) for the water and ⅓ cup (76 g) unsalted butter, melted, for the oil.

The amount of flour can vary depending on the protein moisture content in the grain, so you may need more or less flour to get a soft, slightly sticky dough.

1½ cups	warm water (approx. 110°F / 43°C)	354 g
⅓ cup	oil	75 g
⅓ cup	liquid honey	110 g
2 tsp	salt	12 g
1	egg, optional	1
1 to 2 tbsp	sunflower seed lecithin powder, optional (see page 17)	6 to 12 g
4 to 4½ cups	freshly milled hard wheat flour (approx.), divided (see Tip, left)	580 to 652 g
1 tbsp	quick-rising (instant) yeast	10 g

1. In a large mixing bowl, combine water, oil, honey and salt, plus egg and lecithin powder, if using.

2. Add 3 cups (435 g) flour and mix just until a thick batter forms. Sprinkle yeast over top and continue mixing. While mixing, gradually add just enough remaining flour, ½ cup (72 g) at a time, to form a soft dough.

3. Knead dough until smooth and elastic, 5 to 6 minutes (see page 21). Let rise in a warm place until doubled in bulk, about 1 hour.

4. Punch down dough and turn out onto a lightly floured surface. Divide dough into 2 equal portions. Using your hands, shape into loaves and place in prepared pans. Let rise in a warm place until doubled in bulk, 30 to 45 minutes.

5. While loaves are still rising, preheat oven to 350°F (180°C).

6. Bake in preheated oven for about 30 to 35 minutes until browned and an instant-read thermometer inserted in center of loaf registers at least 190°F (88°C). Remove bread from pans and transfer to a wire rack to cool.

Variations

Bread Bowls: In step 4, divide dough into 4 equal portions. Shape into rounds and place on a parchment paper–lined baking sheet, spacing them apart. Let rise in a warm place until almost doubled in bulk and light and airy, about 30 to 45 minutes. Bake in preheated 350°F (180°C) oven for about 30 minutes or until browned and an instant-read thermometer inserted in center of loaf registers at least 190°F (88°C). Transfer to a wire rack to cool.

To serve as a bowl for soup: Cut a circle in the top of each bread round, slightly cone-shaped, to hollow out the center while leaving a 1-inch (2.5 cm) rim. Lift out circle and pull out the bread from the center of the bread round to form a bowl, leaving a 1-inch (2.5 cm) thick bottom. Ladle soup into bowl and garnish as directed. Serve the pieces pulled from the center of the bread bowl on the side with butter.

French Loaf: In step 4, divide dough into 2 equal portions. Shape each into an oblong loaf, about 12 inches (30 cm) long. Place on a greased French bread pan or baking sheets, spacing them apart. Let rise in a warm place until doubled in bulk, about 30 to 45 minutes. Bake in preheated 375°F (190°C) oven for about 25 to 30 minutes or until browned and an instant-read thermometer inserted in center of loaf registers at least 190°F (88°C). Transfer to a wire rack to cool.

Sandwich Rolls: In step 4, divide dough into 16 pieces, about 2½ oz (70 g) each. Shape into rolls and place on a parchment paper–lined baking sheets, spacing them apart. Let rise in a warm place until doubled in bulk, about 30 to 40 minutes. Bake in preheated 400°F (200°C) oven, one sheet at a time, for about 8 to 10 minutes, until golden brown and an instant-read thermometer inserted in center of rolls registers at least 190°F (88°C). Transfer to a wire rack to cool.

For small dinner rolls, divide dough into 25 pieces, about 1½ oz (42 g) each.

Cheddar-Jalapeño Bread

A simple addition of sharp white Cheddar and a fresh jalapeño to the Basic Yeast Bread dough makes this a perfect bread to serve with a cheesy potato soup or chili. For this variation I like to use 2 parts hard white wheat and 1 part hard red wheat.

MAKES 1 LARGE LOAF

- Ceramic bread cloche, Dutch oven, or cast-iron pot with lid

Tips

If you prefer, this dough can be shaped into 1 free-form round. After shaping in step 2, place on a greased or parchment paper–lined baking sheet (or on the work surface to use a baking stone) and let rise as directed. If desired, place a baking stone in oven while preheating. Bake on baking sheet or directly on preheated baking stone for 30 to 35 minutes or until browned and an instant-read thermometer inserted in center of loaf registers at least 200°F (93°C).

You can also make 2 smaller free-form loaves. After kneading in the cheese and jalapeño, divide the dough into 2 equal portions and shape into 2 balls, then follow directions for the free-form loaf, spacing loaves apart on a prepared baking sheet, if using. Let rise and bake as directed.

1	batch Basic Yeast Bread dough (page 34)	1
2 cups	shredded sharp white Cheddar cheese	224 g
1	jalapeño pepper, seeded and finely chopped	1

1. Prepare Basic Yeast Bread dough. After the first rise (step 3), punch down dough and turn out onto lightly floured work surface. Gently stretch the dough out into a large circle.

2. Sprinkle evenly with cheese and jalapeño. Press into the dough, then pull the dough up and over toward the center and knead to evenly incorporate the cheese and jalapeño. Gently knead into a ball. Let rise in a warm place until light and airy looking, about 30 minutes.

3. Meanwhile, preheat oven to 375°F (190°C). Place bread cloche, Dutch oven or cast-iron pot in oven while preheating.

4. Score the loaf, if desired. Remove cloche base or pot from the oven. Gently lift the loaf onto hot base or into pot. Lightly spritz with water, if desired. Cover with cloche or lid and return to the oven. Bake for 35 to 40 minutes or until browned and an instant-read thermometer inserted in center of loaf registers at least 200°F (93°C). If the loaf needs more browning, remove lid and bake for about 5 minutes, until browned. Transfer bread to a wire rack to cool.

Sun-Dried Tomato, Basil and Garlic Filled Bread

This bread is as visually stunning as it is delicious. You will begin to drool even before the first bite. Enjoy it served alongside a hot bowl of soup, as an appetizer or a quick on-the-go snack.

MAKES TWO 1¼-LB (625 G) LOAVES

- Two large baking sheets, lined with parchment paper, or baking stone (see Tip, below)

Tips

For a milder garlic flavor, use just 1 tbsp (15 g) minced garlic; for a more pronounced garlic flavor, use 2 tbsp (30 g). Or use an amount in between, to your taste.

If using a baking stone, you can let the loaf rise on a sheet of parchment paper on the counter in step 5. Place pizza stone in the oven in step 7 while preheating. Then, using a pizza peel or baking sheet to transfer the loaf on the paper to the stone, slide the parchment paper directly onto the stone to bake.

Use the reserved sun-dried tomato oil as some of the oil in the Basic Yeast Bread dough (with plain oil to make up the needed quantity), for salad dressings or in place of plain olive oil to make croutons.

1	batch Basic Yeast Bread dough (page 34)	1
1	jar (8½ oz / 241 g) oil-packed sun-dried tomatoes	1
1 to 2 tbsp	minced garlic (see Tip, left)	15 to 30 g
2 cups	shredded Italian blend or mozzarella cheese, divided	224 g
⅔ cup	chopped fresh basil	32 g

1. Prepare Basic Yeast Bread dough and let rise as directed in step 3.

2. Meanwhile, drain sun-dried tomatoes, reserving oil for another use. Lay tomatoes on paper towels and pat dry to absorb excess oil. Using kitchen shears or a sharp knife, snip or chop tomatoes into small pieces.

3. After the first rise (step 3), punch down dough and turn onto a lightly floured surface. Divide into 2 equal portions. Working with one portion at a time, roll into a 22- by 8½-inch (55 by 21 cm) rectangle, with a long side facing you.

4. Sprinkle half each of the garlic, to taste, cheese, basil and tomatoes over dough, leaving ½ inch (1 cm) at the top edge free for easy sealing. Starting with the long edge closest to you, roll into a tight cylinder, pressing top edge to seal.

5. Place roll, seam side down, on prepared baking sheet. Using a sharp knife or dough scraper, cut lengthwise down center of roll, about 1 inch (2.5 cm) deep to within ½ inch (1 cm) of the ends. Keeping cut-side up, carefully curve roll to form an S shape; tuck both ends under center of the S to form a figure 8. Pinch ends to seal.

6. Let rise in a warm place until doubled in bulk, about 35 to 40 minutes. Meanwhile, repeat with remaining ingredients to make another loaf.

7. While loaves are still rising, preheat oven to 350°F (180°C).

8. Bake, one loaf at a time, in preheated oven 35 to 40 minutes, tenting with foil after 15 to 20 minutes to prevent overbrowning, until golden brown and an instant-read thermometer inserted in the center of loaf registers at least 190°F (88°C). Remove bread from pan and transfer to a wire rack to cool.

Cheddar Chili Bread Sticks

Another great variation of the Basic Yeast Bread (page 34) dough recipe makes the perfect pairing with a bowl of chili or Tex-Mex inspired dishes like my Creamy Adobo Chicken Soup (page 128).

MAKES 24 BREAD STICKS

- Large baking sheet, greased or lined with parchment paper

Tips

For this recipe, I prefer to use a mild-tasting wheat variety such as hard white or a combination of hard white and Kamut (1:1 or 2:1 hard white to Kamut by volume) in the Basic Yeast Bread dough recipe.

I like to use an all-natural taco seasoning with no MSG, salt or sugar. To easily make your own, in a small bowl, combine 2 tbsp (36 g) chili powder, 5 tsp (10 g) sweet paprika, 4½ tsp (9 g) ground cumin, 1 tbsp (10 g) dried granulated onion, 2½ tsp (7 g) garlic powder, 2 tsp (2 g) dried oregano leaves and ¼ tsp (0.5 g) cayenne pepper; whisk together. Makes about ½ cup (75 g). Store in a jar or airtight container for up to 3 months.

1	batch Basic Yeast Bread dough (page 34, see Tip, left)	1
1½ to 2 cups	shredded Cheddar cheese (6 to 8 oz)	168 to 224 g
1	can (4 oz / 113 g) chopped green chilies, drained	1
2 tbsp	taco seasoning mix (see Tip, left)	18 g
2 to 3 tbsp	olive oil, divided	28 to 42 g
	Grated Parmesan cheese	

GARLIC BUTTER

¼ cup	unsalted butter	57 g
2	cloves garlic, minced	2
Pinch	salt	Pinch

1. Prepare Basic Yeast Bread dough and let rise as directed in step 3.

2. Meanwhile, in a medium bowl, combine cheese, green chilies and taco seasoning. Set aside.

3. After the first rise (step 3), punch down dough and turn onto a lightly floured surface. Divide dough into 2 equal portions. Working with one portion at a time, roll into an 18- by 12-inch (46 by 30 cm) rectangle, with a long side facing you.

4. Using a pastry brush, lightly brush the top half of the rectangle with half of the olive oil. Sprinkle half of the cheese mixture over oil. Fold the bottom half of rectangle (the plain dough) over the top to enclose filling. Press together edges to seal.

5. Using a sharp knife or pizza cutter, cut dough into 12 strips, about 6 inches (15 cm) long by 1½ inches (3.5 cm) wide. Twist each strip several times and place on prepared baking sheet, spacing them apart. Sprinkle tops with Parmesan cheese to taste. Repeat with remaining ingredients. Let rise in a warm place until light and airy looking, about 20 minutes.

6. Meanwhile, preheat oven to 375°F (190°C).

7. Garlic Butter (if using): In a saucepan over low heat, melt butter, garlic and salt, being careful not to let it burn. Remove from heat and let cool until slightly solidified, but still spreadable.

8. Bake for 15 to 20 minutes or until lightly browned. Baste with garlic butter if desired. Serve warm.

Parmesan Pull-Apart Rolls

Yes, you will divide this dough into 48 pieces — that's not a mistake. Think Monkey Bread, only savory. These little pull-apart rolls are buttery, cheesy and absolutely delicious. They were a favorite in one of my soup classes.

MAKES 48 SMALL ROLLS

- Two 9-inch (25 cm) round cake pans

Tip

These rolls are just as delicious reheated. To make ahead, let baked rolls cool completely in the pans on a rack. Remove rolls from pan and wrap in parchment paper and then foil. (I wrap in parchment first, as I do not like my food touching aluminum foil.) Store at room temperature for up to 2 days. When ready to serve, warm wrapped rolls in a preheated 350°F (180°C) oven for about 15 minutes.

1	batch Basic Yeast Bread dough (page 34)	1
2 cups	grated Parmesan cheese	200 g
2 tbsp	dried Italian seasoning	6 g
3/4 cup	unsalted butter, melted	170 g

1. Prepare Basic Yeast Bread dough and let rise as directed in step 3.

2. Meanwhile, in a medium bowl, combine cheese and Italian seasoning. Place melted butter in a small, shallow bowl. Set aside.

3. After the first rise (step 3), punch down dough and turn onto a lightly floured surface. Divide dough into 2 equal portions. Divide each half into 24 equal portions and shape into small balls.

4. Dip each ball of dough in melted butter, then roll in cheese mixture, turning to coat. Arrange evenly spaced in prepared pans with sides touching. Let rise in a warm place until doubled in bulk, about 20 minutes.

5. Meanwhile, preheat oven to 375°F (190°C).

6. Bake for 20 to 30 minutes or until lightly browned and an instant-read thermometer inserted in the center registers at least 190°F (88°C). Let cool slightly in pans on wire racks, then transfer to a serving platter. Serve warm.

Mushroom Cheese Bread

I was served a scrumptious warm bread laden with mushrooms and cheese at a friend's house and asked for the recipe. I simply used my Basic Yeast Bread recipe to make French loaves (see page 35) as a base and then added the savory ingredients as directed. This rich concoction is the perfect pairing for most any soup, making for a very hearty meal. You can change the cheese to any good melting cheese you prefer.

MAKES 12 TO 16 SLICES

- Baking sheet

Tip

Prepare mushroom and cheese mixtures ahead to have on hand to make this a quick dinner or appetizer bread. Store them separately in airtight containers in the refrigerator for up to 2 days. Let warm to room temperature before assembling.

Preheat oven to 350°F (180°C)

2 tbsp	unsalted butter	28 g
6 cups	sliced fresh mushrooms (about 1 lb)	450 g
Pinch	salt	Pinch
4	green onions, chopped	4
2 cups	shredded hot pepper Jack cheese	224 g
1 cup	grated Parmesan cheese	100 g
1 cup	mayonnaise	224 g
1	Basic Yeast Bread French Loaf (see page 35)	1
1	batch Thyme Cheese Spread (left)	1

1. In a large skillet, melt butter over medium-high heat. Add mushrooms and salt; cook, stirring, for about 8 minutes or until tender. Add onions; cook, stirring, for about 3 to 4 minutes or until liquid has evaporated and mushrooms start to brown. Set aside.

2. In a medium bowl, combine hot pepper Jack cheese, Parmesan and mayonnaise. Cut the bread loaf in half lengthwise and then crosswise. Place cut sides up on baking sheet, spacing pieces apart. Spread tops with Thyme Cheese Spread, dividing equally. Spread mayonnaise mixture over top. Spoon mushroom mixture evenly over cheese.

3. Bake for 20 minutes or until the cheese is melted. If desired, broil for 2 to 3 minutes until golden brown. Slice and serve warm.

THYME CHEESE SPREAD

This garlicky cheese spread is perfect on this bread but equally delicious served with crackers and fruit as an appetizer.

In a bowl, combine 8 oz (227 g) softened block-style cream cheese, $\frac{1}{4}$ cup (57 g) softened unsalted butter, 1 clove minced garlic, 2 tsp (2 g) dried thyme leaves, pinch of salt and 1 tsp (5 g) fresh lemon juice; mash well until smooth. Use immediately or store in an airtight container in the refrigerator for up to 2 days. Let warm to room temperature before using. (Makes about 1$\frac{1}{4}$ cups / 295 g.)

Grilled Pimento Cheese Sandwich

My Basic Yeast Bread recipe makes two loaves of lovely sandwich bread, perfect for these grilled cheese sandwiches, so I make sure I always have these loaves on hand. I like to serve these sandwiches with Cream of Tomato Basil Soup. (See photo on page 216.) The cheese spread makes a big batch for you to store in the refrigerator for more sandwiches or spread on crackers for snacking.

MAKES 4 TO 6 SANDWICHES

Tips

Pimentos or pimientos? Both are correct. They are a small, sweet red pepper with a little zip. The chopped peppers in jars are preserved in a salt brine and are the key ingredient for the Southern classic, Pimento Cheese.

Pimientos is the Spanish spelling (in fact, it's the Spanish word for peppers) and is what you'll likely find on the labels.

PIMENTO CHEESE

1	jar (4 oz / 113 g) diced pimentos, drained	1
1 or 2	cloves garlic, minced	1 or 2
¾ cup	mayonnaise	168 g
1 tbsp	ketchup	15 g
1 tsp	Worcestershire sauce	5 g
1 lb	medium Cheddar or Colby cheese, shredded	454 g

SANDWICHES

8 or 12	slices Basic Yeast Bread (page 34)	8 or 12
	Unsalted butter, softened	
2 or 3	tomatoes, sliced, optional	2 or 3

1. **Pimento Cheese:** In a large bowl, combine pimentos, garlic to taste, mayonnaise, ketchup to taste and Worcestershire sauce. Stir in cheese, mashing well to thoroughly combine. Cover and refrigerate for at least 1 hour, until chilled, or for up to 3 days. (Makes about 4 cups / 725 g.)

2. **Sandwiches:** Arrange bread slices in a single layer on a work surface; spread one side of each slice with butter mixture. Flip half of the bread slices over and spread ¼ to ⅓ cup (45 to 60 g) of pimento cheese on top of each. Top with tomato slices, if using. Place remaining bread slices on top with the buttered side out.

3. Heat a large skillet over medium heat. Add sandwiches, in batches as necessary, and cook for about 2 to 3 minutes per side or until browned and cheese is melted, adjusting heat as necessary to avoid burning. Cut sandwiches, as desired, and serve hot.

Orange, Cranberry, Apple Chicken Salad Sandwiches

The sweet and savory flavors in the chicken salad are perfect for any luncheon or dinner. Make them on freshly baked sandwich rolls to accompany Sweet Potato Bisque (page 220) or another light vegetable soup.

MAKES 16 SMALL SANDWICHES

Tips

I like to use some olive oil in this recipe instead of using only mayonnaise. This helps achieve the desired moistness without overpowering it with the flavor of mayonnaise. I especially love to use a blood orange-infused olive oil to boost the orange flavor.

The name of a honey, as well as its color and flavor, is determined by the specific flower from which the nectar was gathered by bees. For this recipe, I love to use an orange blossom honey to enhance the flavor, but any medium or light, floral honey will be delicious.

This recipe makes a lot so can easily be cut in half if it won't be consumed within 3 days.

6	boneless chicken breasts (about 3 lbs / 1.36 kg), cooked and shredded	6
2 to 3 tbsp	dried tarragon leaves	6 to 9 g
½ to 1 cup	mayonnaise	112 to 224 g
2 tbsp	olive oil, optional (see Tip, left)	28 g
2 tbsp	liquid mild honey, preferably orange blossom	42 g
	Grated zest and juice of 1 orange	
1	apple, diced	1
½ cup	dried cranberries	80 g
	Salt, freshly ground black pepper and seasoning salt	
16	Basic Yeast Bread Sandwich Rolls (page 35)	16

1. In a large bowl, combine chicken, 2 tbsp (6 g) of the tarragon, ½ cup (112 g) of the mayonnaise, oil, if using, honey, orange zest and juice, apple and cranberries. Toss to evenly coat. Taste and add more mayonnaise, tarragon, salt, pepper and seasoning salt, to taste. Serve immediately or transfer to an airtight container and refrigerate for up to 3 days.

2. To serve, cut sandwich rolls in half horizontally and fill with chicken salad. Serve immediately.

Crusty No-Knead Bread

This easy no-knead bread will soon become one of your favorites. Crusty on the outside with a soft chewy texture inside, it is the perfect bread to accompany a hot bowl of soup. In fact, I usually call it my "soup bread." Using only 4 basic ingredients, the dough is easy to stir up and, since gluten can develop simply by letting wheat flour fully hydrate, it needs very little hands-on time. Still, full hydration and gluten development takes 6 to 8 hours. So be sure to start the process early in the morning or the night before you want to enjoy it.

MAKES ONE 1½-LB (750 G) LOAF

- Ceramic bread cloche, Dutch oven, or cast-iron pot with lid (see Tip, below)

Tips

A bread cloche, Dutch oven or cast-iron pot with a tight-fitting lid will soon become your best friend. Cooking in a closed round pot gives you the moisture and support you need during baking for free-form and sourdough loaves. The resulting breads will rise higher and have a crispier crust.

When mixing dough in step 1, once the flour is incorporated, you should have a soft, sticky dough that is thick enough to form a ball and pull away from the sides of the bowl. If it is too sticky, gradually add more flour and stir just until it forms a ball. This is a higher hydration dough, so keep in mind the dough should not be as firm as a traditional direct-mix yeast bread.

3 cups	freshly milled hard wheat flour (approx., see Tip, left)	435 g
1¾ tsp	salt	10 g
½ tsp	quick-rising (instant) yeast	2 g
1½ cups	room temperature water	354 g

1. In a large bowl, combine flour, salt and yeast. Add water and stir using a spatula or wooden spoon until all flour is moistened and well incorporated. Cover the bowl with plastic wrap or set a plate on top of the bowl. Let sit for 6 to 8 hours or overnight.

2. I actually prefer to start my dough in the morning and do several "stretch and folds" (see page 51) every hour or so throughout the day. This really improves the gluten strength and gives a better rise to the finished loaf. Do your last stretch and fold about an hour before baking.

3. When ready to bake, preheat oven to 450°F (230°C). Place bread cloche, Dutch oven or cast-iron pot in the oven while preheating.

4. With floured or wet hands, gently remove the dough from the bowl and turn out onto a large piece of floured parchment paper. Using a bench scraper and floured hands, roughly shape into a ball.

5. Gently lift parchment and the shaped ball of dough and drop it into the preheated cloche or pot. Lightly spritz with water, if desired. Replace lid.

6. Bake for 30 minutes. Remove lid and bake another 10 to 15 minutes, until golden brown and an instant-read thermometer inserted in center of loaf registers at least 200°F (93°C). Transfer to a wire rack to cool.

Crusty No-Knead Spelt Bread: Substitute approximately 4½ cups (585 g) freshly milled spelt flour for the hard wheat flour called for in the recipe. If using a cast-iron pot, you may need to reduce the oven temperature to 400°F (200°C) to keep the bottom crust from getting too dark.

STRETCH AND FOLD

This technique, often used in no-knead sourdough, can eliminate the need for kneading. It helps to strengthen and develop the gluten structure in bread dough. Stretch and folds are usually done several times over the course of 6 to 8 hours with 30 minutes to an hour between each one.

Method: Pretend there is a clock face on the surface of your dough. At the 12 o'clock position, gently grab the underside of your dough and stretch it up just enough to fold it over itself. Turn your dough one-quarter turn clockwise and again, at the 12 o'clock position, gently grab the underside of your dough, stretch it up and fold it over the dough. Repeat two more times, turning the dough clockwise a quarter turn each time. This completes one stretch and fold.

Variations

About 1 hour before baking or with the last stretch and fold, you can change the flavor of the bread by trying one of these add-in combinations.

Prune-Feta-Rosemary: Reduce salt in the main recipe to 1¼ tsp (8 g). When ready to shape, add ½ to ¾ cup (93 to 139 g) prunes, snipped into small pieces, ½ cup (75 g) crumbled feta cheese, 2 tbsp (20 g) dark unrefined cane sugar, and 2 tbsp (4 g) minced fresh rosemary to the dough. Knead gently to incorporate. Shape as desired. Let rest about 15 minutes while oven preheats. Bake as directed.

Cheddar and Herb: When ready to shape, add 8 oz (227 g) sharp (old) Cheddar cheese, grated (or more, if desired), and 1 to 2 tbsp (3 to 6 g) of your favorite dried herb combination (oregano, basil, thyme, rosemary) to the dough. (I use a dried Italian seasoning blend.) Knead gently to incorporate. Shape as desired. Let rest about 30 minutes while oven preheats. Bake 35 minutes with the lid on. Remove lid and bake about 15 more minutes, until internal temperature reaches 200°F (93°C).

Give It Some Heat Cheese Jalapeño: When ready to shape, add 8 oz (227 g) hot pepper Jack cheese, shredded (or more, if desired), and 1 finely diced fresh jalapeño (seeds removed) to the dough. Knead gently to incorporate. Shape as desired. Let rest about 30 minutes while oven preheats. Bake 35 minutes with the lid on. Remove lid and bake about 15 more minutes, until internal temperature reaches 200°F (93°C).

Crusty No-Knead Sourdough Bread

Because I love how easy it is to make my Crusty No-Knead Bread, and I love sourdough, I wanted to combine the two. And tada — we have a crusty no-knead sourdough! Be sure to feed your starter 8 to 10 hours before you begin so it's bubbly and active when you're ready to prepare the dough, and also allow 6 to 8 hours before baking for full hydration of the flour and gluten development.

MAKES ONE 1½-LB (750 G) LOAF

- Ceramic bread cloche, Dutch oven, or cast-iron pot with lid (see Tip, page 48)

Tips

There are many ways to get a sourdough starter: you can make your own (there are recipes widely available); you can mail-order a fresh or dehydrated starter; some baking supply shops and restaurants sell it; and, if you have any friends or family who make sourdough, they're usually more than willing to give you some and welcome you into the wonderful world of sourdough making!

When mixing dough in step 1, once the flour is incorporated, you should have a soft, sticky dough that is thick enough to form a ball and pull away from the sides of the bowl. If it is too sticky, gradually add more flour and stir just until it forms a ball. This is a higher hydration dough, so keep in mind that the dough should not be as firm as a traditional direct-mix yeast bread.

1½ cups	room temperature water	354 g
½ cup	bubbly active sourdough starter (see Tip, left)	115 g
3 cups	freshly milled hard wheat flour (approx., see Tip, left)	435 g
1¾ tsp	salt	10 g

1. In a large bowl, combine water and sourdough starter. Add flour and salt and stir using a spatula or wooden spoon until all flour is moistened and well incorporated. Cover the bowl with plastic wrap or set a plate on top of the bowl. Let sit for 6 to 8 hours or overnight.

2. I actually prefer to start my dough in the morning and do several "stretch and folds" (see instructions on page 51) every hour or so throughout the day. This really improves the gluten strength and gives a better rise to the finished loaf. Do your last stretch and fold about an hour before baking.

3. When ready to bake, preheat oven to 450°F (230°C). Place bread cloche, Dutch oven or cast-iron pot in the oven while preheating.

4. With floured or wet hands, gently remove the dough from the bowl and turn out onto a large piece of floured parchment paper. Using a bench scraper and floured hands, roughly shape into a ball.

5. Gently lift parchment and the shaped ball of dough and drop it into the preheated cloche or pot. Lightly spritz with water, if desired. Replace lid.

6. Bake for 30 minutes. Remove lid and bake another 10 to 15 minutes, until golden brown and an instant-read thermometer inserted in the center of loaf registers at least 200°F (93°C). Transfer to a wire rack to cool.

Rye Bread

This recipe for traditional rye bread is a slight variation on the Basic Yeast Bread. Vinegar adds a tangy flavor but also keeps the dough from being too sticky. Gluten and lecithin are always optional, but they will improve the texture and rise of the bread. Using the sponge method will help strengthen the gluten structure of the rye flour. Do not over-knead! Shape this dough into baguettes to make small rounds for the Grilled Swiss on Rye Sandwiches for the Patty Melt Soup (pages 180 to 183).

MAKES ONE 2-LB (1 KG) LOAF

- Baking sheet, greased or lined with parchment paper

Tips

If using a machine to knead the dough, be careful not to over-knead. Rye flour has weak gluten potential and can easily break down if kneaded too much. Stop kneading as soon as the dough begins to form a nice smooth ball and looks shiny. Dough that has been kneaded too long will get very wet and sticky-looking again. See page 21 for bread machine instructions.

If making freeform loaves, let them rise (step 4) at room temperature rather than in a warm place. Proofing at too warm a temperature will cause the loaves to spread out instead of rising up into a nice rounded loaf.

1½ cups	warm water (approx. 110°F / 43°C)	354 g
2 cups	freshly milled rye flour	270 g
1 tbsp	quick-rising (instant) yeast	10 g
⅓ cup	oil	75 g
⅓ cup	liquid honey	110 g
2 tbsp	cider vinegar or white balsamic vinegar	30 g
2 tsp	salt	12 g
1 to 2 tbsp	caraway seeds	7 to 14 g
1	egg, optional	1
1 tbsp	sunflower seed lecithin powder, optional (see page 17)	6 g
1 tsp	vital wheat gluten, optional	3 g
2 to 2½ cups	freshly milled hard wheat flour	290 to 362 g

1. In a large mixing bowl, combine water, rye flour and yeast, stirring well to form a sponge. Set aside at room temperature for about 10 to 15 minutes.

2. Add oil, honey, vinegar, salt and caraway seeds, plus egg, lecithin powder and gluten, if using, and mix well. While mixing, gradually add just enough wheat flour, ½ cup (72 g) at a time, to form a soft dough.

3. Knead dough until smooth and elastic, 3 to 5 minutes. Let rise in a warm place until doubled in bulk, about 1 hour.

4. Punch down dough and turn out onto a lightly floured or oiled surface. Shape into a round loaf. Place on prepared baking sheet. Let rise at room temperature until light and airy, 30 minutes.

5. While loaf is still rising, preheat oven to 350°F (180°C).

6. Bake in preheated oven for 30 to 35 minutes, until golden brown and an instant-read thermometer inserted in the center registers at least 190°F (88°C). Remove bread from pan and transfer to a wire rack to cool.

Variations

Rye Baguettes: In step 4, divide dough into 3 equal portions. Shape each into a 14-inch (35 cm) long baguette. Place in a baguette pan or onto a large parchment paper–lined baking sheet, spacing loaves apart. Let rise as directed, for about 20 minutes. Preheat oven to 375°F (190°C) and reduce baking time to 20 to 25 minutes.

Rye Sandwich Loaf: To make two 1-lb (500 g) sandwich-style loaves, in step 4, divide dough into 2 equal portions and shape each into a loaf. Place into two 8- by 4-inch (20 by 10 cm) greased or parchment paper–lined loaf pans. Let rise, preheat oven and bake as directed in steps 4, 5 and 6.

Dark Molasses Sweet Bread

My goal with this recipe was to create a healthy copycat version of the bread served at a popular steakhouse. Sweet with an earthy flavor of molasses, this bread served warm with Homemade Garlic Honey Butter (page 59) is delicious.

MAKES 4 SMALL FREEFORM LOAVES

- Large baking sheet, greased or lined with parchment paper (optional)
- Baking stone, optional

Tips

You can use ¼ cup (60 g) pure maple syrup or ¼ cup (84 g) agave nectar in place of the honey.

If using a baking stone, you can let the loaves rise on a sheet of parchment paper on the counter in step 4. Then, using a pizza peel or baking sheet to transfer the loaves on the paper to the stone, slide the parchment paper directly onto the stone to bake. Depending on the size of your stone, you may need to bake the loaves in batches to avoid crowding for a better crust

¾ cup	large-flake (old-fashioned) rolled oats	86 g
¼ cup	unsalted butter, cut into pieces, softened	57 g
1¼ cups	hot water	295 g
2 tbsp	unsweetened cocoa powder	12 g
2½ tsp	salt	14 g
½ cup	milk	120 g
¼ cup	liquid honey (see Tip, left)	82 g
¼ cup	unsulfured blackstrap molasses	84 g
4½ cups	freshly milled hard wheat flour	652 g
1½ tbsp	quick-rising (instant) yeast	15 g
1	egg white	1
1 tbsp	water	15 g
	Additional large-flake (old-fashioned) rolled oats	

1. In a large mixing bowl, combine oats and butter; pour in hot water. Let stand for 5 minutes. Add cocoa powder, salt, milk, honey and molasses and mix well.

2. Add 3 cups (435 g) flour and mix until a thick batter forms. Sprinkle yeast over top and continue mixing. While mixing, gradually add just enough remaining flour, ½ cup (72 g) at a time, to form a soft dough.

3. Knead dough until smooth and elastic, 5 to 6 minutes. Let rise in a warm place until doubled in bulk, about 1 hour.

4. Punch down dough and turn out onto a lightly floured or oiled surface. Divide dough into 4 equal portions. Shape each into a small oblong loaf, about 9 inches (23 cm) long. Place on prepared baking sheet (see Tip, left), spacing them apart. Let rise in a warm place until light and airy, about 20 minutes.

5. While loaves are still rising, preheat oven to 375°F (190°C). If using a baking stone, place in oven while preheating.

6. In a small bowl, whisk egg white with water. Using a pastry brush, evenly brush risen loaves with egg white wash and sprinkle with additional rolled oats.

7. Bake for 30 minutes or until browned and an instant-read thermometer inserted in the center registers 200°F (93°C). Remove bread from pan and transfer to a wire rack to cool.

Homemade Garlic Honey Butter

There is nothing much better than a piece of warm homemade bread slathered with butter, except perhaps that same bread slathered with homemade butter. And this sweet garlic butter is absolutely delicious on a warm roll or piece of bread — especially the Dark Molasses Sweet Bread.

MAKES 1 CUP (227 G) BUTTER

- Stand mixer with whip attachment

Tip

You can use the reserved buttermilk as the milk in a yeast bread dough recipe or as the liquid in a quick bread if you want to add a honey and garlic flavor. The buttermilk can be stored in a sealed jar in the refrigerator for up to 2 days.

2 cups	heavy or whipping (35%) cream	480 g
2 tbsp	liquid honey	42 g
2 to 3 tbsp	minced garlic	30 to 45 g
Pinch	salt	Pinch

1. In a medium bowl or 1-qt (1 L) jar, combine cream, honey and garlic, stirring or swirling jar until honey is dissolved. Cover and refrigerate for at least 1 hour, until well chilled, or for up to 1 day.

2. Pour cream mixture into stand mixer bowl and fit with whip attachment. Mix on lowest speed, then gradually increase speed to high. Whip vigorously (fitting a bowl lid into place, if available, or holding a tea towel carefully around bowl to prevent splashing). The cream will form soft peaks, then firm peaks, then will slowly begin to break back down with the butter solids separating from the buttermilk. Continue whipping until butter solids have combined into large clumps.

3. Turn mixer off. Using a slotted spoon, lift butter solids into a clean bowl. Take a flat spatula and press the butter solids repeatedly to remove any additional buttermilk, pouring the liquid into the bowl of buttermilk as it's released from the butter. Reserve buttermilk for another use (see Tip, left). Once all the liquid has been pressed out of the butter solids, transfer butter to a small bowl.

4. Add a pinch of salt to taste and mash with the spatula to incorporate into the butter completely. Serve immediately, or form into a log and wrap in plastic and store in the refrigerator for up to 3 days. Or you can place log in a freezer bag or airtight container and freeze for several months.

Buttermilk Potato Bread

The grated raw potatoes in this dough help the bread to rise and give a wonderful moist texture and subtle flavor that will make this bread a favorite served warm with a hot bowl of soup.

MAKE ONE 2½-LB (1.25 KG) OR TWO 1¼-LB (625 G) ROUND LOAVES

- Box-style cheese grater
- Medium heavy saucepan
- One or two baking sheets (see Tip, below)

Tips

Baking this bread in a ceramic bread cloche, Dutch oven or cast-iron with lid gives it a really nice crisp crust with a moist crumb inside. Place cloche, Dutch oven or pot in oven while preheating as directed in step 6. Shape into 1 round loaf and let rest for 15 minutes on a floured work surface or on a sheet of parchment paper. When ready to bake, carefully lift loaf or paper and place in preheated cloche or pot. Spritz with water. Cover with the lid. Bake for 35 to 40 minutes until browned and an instant-read thermometer inserted in the center registers 200°F (93°C). If the loaf needs more browning, remove lid and bake for about 5 minutes, until browned. Transfer bread to a wire rack to cool.

The amount of flour can vary depending on the protein moisture content in the grain, so you may need more or less flour to get a soft, slightly sticky dough.

2	medium potatoes (about 1 lb / 454 g)	2
1½ cups	buttermilk	360 g
¼ cup	water	59 g
1 tbsp	salt	18 g
4¾ cups	freshly milled hard wheat flour (approx., see Tip, left)	689 g
1 tbsp	quick-rising (instant) yeast	10 g
	Unsalted butter	
	Cornmeal (optional)	

1. Peel potatoes and rinse under running water. Grate on the coarse side of cheese grater. In a saucepan, combine potatoes, buttermilk, water and salt; heat over low heat until lukewarm.

2. Pour the warmed mixture into a large mixing bowl. Add 3 cups (435 g) flour and mix just until a thick batter forms. Sprinkle yeast over top and continue mixing. While mixing, gradually add just enough remaining flour, ½ cup (72 g) at a time, to form a soft dough.

3. Knead dough until smooth and elastic, 5 to 6 minutes. Let rise in a warm place until doubled in bulk, about 1 hour.

4. Meanwhile, butter baking sheet(s) and sprinkle with cornmeal, if using.

5. Punch down dough and turn out onto a lightly floured or oiled surface. Shape into 1 large round loaf or 2 small round loaves. Place on prepared baking pan, spacing loaves apart if making 2, and let rise in a warm place until doubled in bulk, about 25 to 30 minutes.

6. While loaf or loaves are still rising, preheat oven to 375°F (190°C).

7. Bake in preheated oven for 30 to 35 minutes until browned and an instant-read thermometer inserted in the center registers 200°F (93°C). Remove bread from pan and transfer to a wire rack to cool.

Ciabatta Bread

Ciabatta is a chewy, slightly crusty traditional Italian bread, perfect to serve alongside a bowl of soup. Its rustic shape gives it character, so don't stress over making each piece perfectly shaped.

MAKES 4 SMALL LOAVES

- Large baking sheet
- Rolling mat

Tips

To make the dough in a bread machine, add ingredients to the pan in the order listed. Set on the Dough cycle; let machine mix and knead for 20 minutes. Remove dough from machine and proceed with step 2 as directed.

I prefer hard white wheat for this recipe because it has a milder flavor and color, but hard red wheat will work as well.

To make 8 smaller ciabatta: In step 3, on the rolling mat, dust the dough liberally with flour then pat it into a rectangle, about 10 by 7 inches (25 by 18 cm). It doesn't have to be exact; that's part of the character of ciabatta. Using a bench scraper, cut the rectangle into 8 equal pieces. Let rise and bake as directed (check for doneness earlier, after about 15 minutes).

1½ cups	warm water (approx. 110°F / 43°C)	354 g
1½ tsp	salt	9 g
1 tsp	liquid honey	7 g
1 tbsp	olive oil	14 g
3¼ cups	freshly milled hard white wheat flour (see Tip, left)	471 g
1½ tsp	quick-rising (instant) yeast	6 g
	Oil	
	Additional freshly milled hard white wheat flour	

1. In a large mixing bowl, combine water, salt, honey, oil, flour and yeast. Knead until dough is smooth and elastic, for 5 to 6 minutes. Cover and let rise for 15 minutes.

2. Meanwhile, preheat oven to 425°F (220°C).

3. Dust baking sheet lightly with flour. Turn dough onto oiled rolling mat. Divide into 4 equal pieces and gently shape into squares. (A dough scraper helps with this.) Place loaves on floured baking sheet, spacing them apart, and lightly dust with flour. Let rise in warm place for about 15 minutes until lightly puffed. (They will continue to rise in the oven.)

4. Spritz loaves lightly with water. Bake in preheated oven for 20 minutes, until golden brown. Remove bread from pan and transfer to a wire rack to cool.

Variation

Spelt Ciabatta Bread: Substitute 4 cups (520 g) freshly milled spelt flour for the hard white wheat flour.

Authentic Pan Pita

On a trip to Israel, where the most common flatbread is pita, I enjoyed pita every day for lunch filled with delicious falafel, cucumber, and other fresh vegetables. We were also served pita that we cooked over an open fire on a hot skillet served with olive oil and Za'atar, a favorite spice blend used in Israel.

MAKES EIGHT 5- TO 6-INCH (12.5 TO 15 CM) PITA

- Nonstick or cast-iron skillet or griddle with lid

Tips

You can use about $3\frac{1}{2}$ cups (507 g) freshly milled hard whole wheat flour for the spelt flour.

To make this dough in a bread machine, add ingredients to the pan in the order listed. Set on the Dough cycle; let machine mix and knead for 15 to 20 minutes. Remove dough from machine and proceed with step 2 as directed.

Oven Variation

While dough balls rest in step 3, preheat oven to 500°F (250°C); place baking stone in oven as it preheats. Proceed with step 4. Place pita rounds on hot baking stone, in batches as necessary. Bake, uncovered, for about 4 minutes until browned. Remove rounds from the oven, cover with a towel or place in plastic bag while other pita rounds bake. Let oven return to heat between batches as necessary.

$1\frac{3}{4}$ cup	warm water (110°F / 43°C)	413 g
$1\frac{1}{2}$ tbsp	liquid honey	32 g
1 tbsp	salt	18 g
$4\frac{1}{2}$ cups	freshly milled spelt flour (approx., see Tip, left)	585 g
$2\frac{1}{2}$ tsp	quick-rising (instant) yeast	9 g

1. In a large mixing bowl, combine water, honey, salt, flour and yeast. Knead until a smooth dough forms, about 5 minutes, kneading in more flour, if necessary, to make a soft, not sticky dough.

2. Cover and let rise in a warm place until a little less than doubled in bulk, about 30 minutes.

3. Punch down dough and turn out onto lightly floured surface. Divide into 8 equal portions and shape each into a ball, flattening slightly with hands as you shape into balls. Leave on work surface, cover with a tea towel and let rest for about 30 to 40 minutes.

4. Working with one ball at a time, on the lightly floured work surface, roll out into a $\frac{1}{4}$-inch (5 mm) thick round, about 5 to 6 inches (12.5 to 15 cm) in diameter. (Roll the remaining pita while you cook.)

5. Heat a nonstick or cast-iron skillet or griddle over high heat until very hot, but not smoking. Reduce the heat to medium-high. Add 1 round of dough and cover immediately. Cook for 2 to 3 minutes until the bottom is browned. (Check often on the first round, to determine if the pan is adequately heated and how long it will take — you do not want the pita to burn.) Flip the pita over, cover and cook for 1 to 2 minutes, until the second side is pale brown. Remove to a plate and cover with towel or plastic bag to keep moist.

6. Repeat with remaining pita, stacking them on top of each other as they are cooked and keeping covered. Adjust heat as necessary between batches to prevent burning. Serve warm.

Indian Naan

Naan is a traditional yeast-leavened flat bread typically cooked in a clay oven. I use a preheated clay baking stone in my oven to capture similar baking results. These require a long rest, so be sure to prepare the dough at least 8 hours before you plan to cook.

MAKES ABOUT TEN 9- BY 7-INCH (23 BY 18 CM) NAAN

- Baking peel or rimless baking sheet
- Large baking stone

2 cups	warm water (approx. 110°F / 43°C)	472 g
1 cup	milk	240 g
4 tsp	salt	24 g
6 to 7 cups	freshly milled spelt flour (approx., see Tip, left)	780 to 910 g
1 tsp	quick-rising (instant) yeast	4 g
	Oil	
3 to 4 tbsp	unsalted butter, melted	42 to 57 g
	Everything bagel seasoning (see Tip, left), optional	

1. In a large mixing bowl, combine water, milk and salt. Add 3 cups (390 g) flour and mix just until a thick batter forms. Sprinkle yeast over top and continue mixing. While mixing, gradually add just enough remaining flour, ½ cup (65 g) at a time, to form a soft dough.

2. Knead dough until smooth and elastic, about 5 minutes. The dough should be soft and just slightly sticky; knead in a little more flour, if necessary. Place dough in an oiled bowl and turn to coat the dough with oil. Cover and let it rise in a cool place for 8 hours or overnight (see Tip, left).

3. Preheat oven to 500°F (250°C). Place baking stone on an upper-middle rack while preheating.

4. Punch down dough and turn out onto a lightly floured surface. Divide the dough in half. Keep half covered while you work with the other. Cut the dough half into 5 equal pieces. Shape each piece into a smooth round ball, using your hand to roll and pinch a tight skin around the ball. Place the rounds of dough on a baking sheet or set aside on the counter. Using a pastry brush, lightly coat each with melted butter. Cover with plastic wrap and let rest for about 20 minutes.

Tips

You can use 4⅔ to 5½ (677 to 797 g) approx. freshly milled hard wheat flour in place of the spelt flour.

You can buy a prepared everything bagel seasoning or make your own with equal parts mixture of dried minced garlic, dried minced onion, sesame seeds and poppy seeds.

At the end of step 2, if you are not ready to bake it yet, you can punch down the dough down and put it in an airtight container or bag and refrigerate for up to 3 days. Let warm to room temperature before shaping.

These are best enjoyed the day they are baked. Let any leftovers cool completely on a wire rack then freeze in an airtight container for up to 1 month. Let thaw, then reheat in a preheated 350°F (180°C) oven for about 5 minutes before serving.

5. During the last few minutes of resting, shape the remaining dough the same way to make 5 more balls and let rest. While this half rests, shape the first half for baking.

6. Working with one ball of dough, on a lightly floured work surface, gently stretch and push it out with your fingertips to a 6- to 7-inch (15 to 18 cm) round. Set it aside to relax and repeat with a second ball. Return to the first piece and stretch it out to an oval about 9 by 7 inches (23 cm by 18 cm) — it is easiest if you pick the dough up and allow it to drape over the back of your hand, pulling it gently to stretch it without poking holes in the dough. Place the stretched oval on a peel or a rimless baking sheet lightly dusted with flour. Repeat with the second piece. Sprinkle with everything bagel seasoning, if using. Shape remaining breads, in batches, as you bake.

7. Working quicky and carefully, slide breads off the peel or baking sheet directly onto the hot baking stone. Bake in preheated oven for about 5 to 6 minutes, until puffy, blistered and lightly browned. Transfer to a plate and baste with additional butter, if desired. Cover with towel to keep warm while baking the rest. Stack breads as they come out of the oven. Let oven return to heat between batches as necessary.

8. Serve warm.

Cornbread

When I think of soup, I usually think of cornbread. My Southern roots are showing. You simply can't go wrong with a nice slice of warm cornbread smeared with butter alongside your chili or favorite soup. It's a classic combination.

MAKES 8 TO 10 SERVINGS

- 10-inch (25 cm) cast-iron skillet or 8- or 9-inch (20 or 23 cm) square baking pan

Tips

True Southern cornbread omits the sweetener (in this case, honey) and uses only cornmeal.

If desired, substitute 1½ cups (263 g) freshly milled coarsely ground cornmeal or corn flour for the wheat flour and cornmeal combination in this recipe.

Freshly milled white or yellow corn or even popcorn makes great cornbread. Corn should be ground on the coarsest setting of the flour mill. Some electric flour mills produce fairly fine flour even on the coarsest setting. To give it a little more "grit" and a cornmeal texture, mill popcorn instead of dent corn.

Preheat oven to 400°F (200°C)

6 tbsp	unsalted butter, cut into pieces	85 g
¾ cup	freshly milled soft wheat flour	94 g
¾ cup	freshly milled coarsely ground cornmeal or corn flour (see Tips, left)	131 g
2½ tsp	baking powder	12 g
¾ tsp	salt	5 g
1	egg, beaten	1
¾ cup	milk	180 g
2 tbsp	liquid honey, optional	42 g

1. Add butter to cast-iron skillet or pan and place in oven to melt while preheating, being careful not to let the butter burn.

2. Meanwhile, in a large bowl, whisk together soft wheat flour, cornmeal, baking powder and salt. Make a well in the center.

3. Add egg, milk and honey (if using) all at once to flour mixture and stir just until all ingredients are moistened. Add melted butter from skillet, leaving about 2 tbsp (14 g) in skillet to cover the bottom of the pan. Stir just until combined. Immediately pour batter into hot skillet.

4. Bake in preheated oven for 20 to 25 minutes, until golden brown and firm to the touch.

Peppery Cheese Bread

A cheesy bread with a peppery kick makes a great accompaniment to any soup. Vary the amount of pepper to your taste.

MAKES 1 LOAF

- 8- by 4-inch (20 by 10 cm) loaf pan, greased

Tips

Change the flavor by using different cheeses. For an extra peppery kick, use hot pepper Jack, and for a mild flavor, use Colby or plain Monterey Jack. If it's a cheese that shreds and melts well, it will work well in this bread.

Any leftovers can be cooled completely, then wrapped tightly or placed in an airtight container to store in the refrigerator for up to 3 days.

Preheat oven to 350°F (180°C)

3 cups	freshly milled soft white wheat flour	375 g
1½ to 2 tsp	cracked black pepper	3 to 4 g
1 tsp	baking powder	5 g
¾ tsp	salt	5 g
½ tsp	baking soda	3 g
2	eggs	2
1 cup	plain yogurt	240 g
½ cup	oil	114 g
¼ cup	milk	60 g
1 tbsp	liquid honey	21 g
1 tbsp	spicy brown mustard	15 g
1 cup	shredded medium or sharp Cheddar cheese	112 g
¼ cup	thinly sliced green onions	25 g

1. In a large bowl, whisk together flour, pepper to taste, baking powder, salt and baking soda. Make a well in the center.
2. In a medium bowl, whisk together eggs, yogurt, oil, milk, honey and mustard. Add to flour mixture; sprinkle in cheese and green onions. Stir just until all ingredients are moistened. Pour batter into prepared pan.
3. Bake in preheated oven for 45 to 50 minutes or until a toothpick inserted in center comes out clean. Let cool in pan for 10 minutes. Remove from pan and transfer to wire rack to let cool slightly. Serve warm.

Corn and Jalapeño Jack Cheese Waffles

I prefer a mild-flavored white corn for these waffles so that all the flavors of the cheese, corn and jalapeños shine through. They are a real crowd pleaser when served with chili. You can make them ahead or just before serving — the hot chili will easily warm up the waffles.

MAKES ABOUT 16 TO 20 WAFFLES

Tips

You can also use a combination of $1\frac{1}{2}$ cups (210 g) freshly milled corn flour and $1\frac{1}{2}$ cups (188 g) freshly milled soft wheat flour for a softer texture in the waffles.

If you don't have any buttermilk on hand, for each cup (240 g) you need, add 1 tbsp (15 g) white or cider vinegar or lemon juice to milk or a non-dairy alternative (almond, rice, soy or coconut milk). Measure the vinegar or lemon juice directly into a measuring cup (or bowl on a kitchen scale), then add enough milk to make 1 cup (240 g). Set aside for about 5 minutes, until slightly thickened.

You can change up the flavor of these waffles by using infused olive oils, like one with Southwest spices to serve with chili, or garlic- or herb-infused oil to match the flavor of other soups.

Preheat waffle iron

3 cups	freshly milled corn flour (see Tip, left)	420 g
$2\frac{1}{2}$ tsp	baking powder	12 g
1 tsp	salt	6 g
1 tsp	baking soda	6 g
4	eggs, beaten	4
$\frac{1}{2}$ cup	olive oil (see Tip, left)	114 g
3 to 4 cups	buttermilk	720 to 960 g
2 cups	shredded jalapeño or hot pepper Jack cheese (about 8 oz)	224 g
1 cup	whole kernel corn (thawed if frozen)	135 g
1 tbsp	chopped jalapeño peppers, optional	11 g

1. In a large bowl, whisk together flour, baking powder, salt and baking soda. Make a well in the center.
2. Add eggs, oil and 3 cups (720 g) buttermilk all at once to flour mixture. Stir just until all ingredients are combined, adding more buttermilk to make a thick, but pourable batter. Fold in cheese, corn and jalapeño (if using).
3. Cook on preheated waffle iron according to manufacturer's instructions. Serve immediately or let cool on a wire rack.

Cheddar Corn Jalapeño Muffins

This is one of our favorite savory muffin variations and it goes well with any soup or dinner.

MAKES 12 MUFFINS OR 24 TO 30 MINI MUFFINS

- 12-cup muffin pan or 24-cup mini muffin pan, greased or lined with papers (see Tip, below)

Tips

You may need to add up to 6 additional muffin cups if making mini muffins.

I prefer to use white dent corn for these cheesy muffins. White corn has a mild flavor so allows the flavors of the cheese and peppers to come through. Dent corn, when milled into flour, has a softer, more flour-like texture than milled popcorn.

If you don't have any buttermilk on hand, add 1 tbsp (15 g) white or cider vinegar or lemon juice to milk or a non-dairy alternative (almond, rice, soy or coconut milk). Measure the vinegar or lemon juice directly into a measuring cup (or bowl on a kitchen scale), then add enough milk to make 1 cup (240 g). Set aside for about 5 minutes, until slightly thickened.

Preheat oven to 400°F (200°C)

2¼ cups	freshly milled corn flour (see Tip, left)	315 g
1 tsp	baking powder	5 g
1 tsp	baking soda	6 g
1 tsp	salt	6 g
1	egg	1
1 cup	buttermilk	240 g
½ cup	oil	114 g
¼ cup	liquid honey	82 g
2 cups	shredded Cheddar or hot pepper Jack cheese (about 8 oz)	224 g
1 cup	fresh or frozen whole kernel corn	135 g
1	small jalapeño pepper, seeds removed, finely chopped, optional	1

1. In a large bowl, whisk together flour, baking powder, baking soda and salt. Make a well in the center.
2. In another bowl, whisk together egg, buttermilk, oil and honey. Add all at once to flour mixture. Stir together just until dry ingredients are moistened. Fold in cheese, corn and jalapeño (if using).
3. Divide batter equally among prepared muffin cups, filling three-quarters full. Bake in preheated oven for 20 minutes (15 minutes for mini muffins), until golden brown and tops spring back when lightly touched.

Easy Drop Biscuits

This drop biscuit recipe is one of my favorites, especially when I am short on time and need a good bread to go with our meal or soup of the day. It uses oil, so there is no need for cutting in butter, making them quick and easy to prepare. Soft wheat will give these biscuits a moist crumb, but other grains, such as barley or a combination of grains, may be used as well. No kneading or rolling is required — simply drop the batter onto the baking sheet or hot stone and bake!

MAKES 1 DOZEN

- Baking sheet, greased, or preheated baking stone

Tips

For a dairy-free version, use almond milk, soy milk or coconut milk.

For a richer, nuttier flavor and increased fiber, replace the soft wheat flour with 2 cups (200 g) barley flour.

If you're using a baking stone, you can scoop the batter directly onto the hot stone without removing it from the oven. Working carefully, simply slide out the oven rack with the stone on it and portion out the batter onto the hot stone, working quickly, so the oven does not cool down too much. Slide the rack back into the oven and bake as directed.

Preheat oven to 425°F (220°C)

2½ cups	freshly milled soft wheat flour	313 g
1 tbsp	baking powder	15 g
1 tsp	salt	6 g
¼ cup	oil	57 g
1 cup	milk or non-dairy alternative (see Tip, left)	240 g

1. In a large bowl, whisk together flour, baking powder and salt. Make a well in the center.

2. In another bowl, whisk together oil and milk. Add all at once to flour mixture and stir just until combined.

3. Using an ice-cream scoop or tablespoon, drop batter onto prepared baking sheet or preheated stone, spacing about 2 inches (5 cm) apart (see Tip, left).

4. Bake in preheated oven for 10 minutes, until golden brown. Let cool on baking sheet for 5 minutes, then transfer to a wire rack to cool further. Serve warm or at room temperature.

Dill and Feta Cheese Drop Biscuits

Dill and feta cheese are two of my favorite flavors to incorporate into most any bread, and I've added both to this easy drop biscuit. I have adapted this very easy and versatile biscuit dough for both savory and sweet biscuits. Try adding different shredded cheese and herbs for other savory flavors or stirring in cinnamon and nutmeg with a little extra sweetness for an easy breakfast biscuit.

MAKES 1 DOZEN

- Baking sheet, greased, or preheated baking stone

Tip

If you have one, a baking stone is great for baking biscuits (see page 76). The biscuits will rise higher than when baked on a traditional baking sheet.

Preheat oven to 425°F (220°C)

2½ cups	freshly milled soft wheat flour	313 g
1 tbsp	baking powder	15 g
1 tsp	salt	6 g
¼ cup	olive oil	57 g
1 cup	milk	240 g
1 cup	crumbled feta cheese	150 g
2 tbsp	chopped fresh dill	6 g

1. In a large bowl, whisk together flour, baking powder and salt. Make a well in the center.

2. In another bowl, whisk together oil and milk. Add all at once to flour mixture, along with feta and dill. Stir just until combined.

3. Using an ice-cream scoop or tablespoon, drop batter onto prepared baking sheet or preheated stone, spacing about 2 inches (5 cm) apart (see Tips, left and page 56).

4. Bake in preheated oven for 10 minutes, until golden brown. Let cool on baking sheet for 5 minutes, then transfer to a wire rack to cool further. Serve warm or at room temperature.

Butter Swim Biscuits

These buttermilk biscuits are baked "swimming" in butter, hence the name. This is an old Southern recipe that I converted using freshly milled soft wheat flour, creating a buttery crusted biscuit that is soft and delicious on the inside. It's one of my favorites with a bowl of Sue's Chuckwagon Beef Stew (page 258), or really most anything. Leftover biscuits are delicious toasted with butter for breakfast or dinner the next day.

MAKES 9 OR 16 BISCUITS

Tip

Soft white wheat is my preference for this recipe. The milder flavor of the white wheat compared to red wheat lets the butter be the highlight. The softer, plumper kernels and lower protein of the soft wheat make for more tender biscuits than you'd get with hard wheat.

Preheat oven to 450°F (230°C)

½ cup	unsalted butter, cut into pieces	114 g
3 cups	freshly milled soft white wheat flour	375 g
4 tsp	baking powder	20 g
2 tsp	salt	12 g
1 tbsp	honey granules or granulated cane sugar, optional	10 g
2 cups	buttermilk	480 g

1. Place butter in baking pan. Place pan in oven to melt butter for about 5 minutes, making sure it doesn't burn.

2. In a medium bowl, whisk together flour, baking powder, salt and honey granules (if using). Make a well in the center. Add buttermilk all at once and stir together just until dry ingredients are moistened and a wet dough forms.

3. Remove baking pan from oven. Pour dough over melted butter and, using a spatula, spread it evenly across the pan until it touches the sides of the pan. Do not mix the butter in. Using a knife, cut through the unbaked dough into 9 or 16 even squares. The dough is now swimming in butter.

4. Bake in preheated oven for 20 to 25 minutes or until golden brown and tops spring back when lightly touched. Let cool slightly in pan. Recut squares to lift out of pan and serve warm.

Dubliner Cheese and Caramelized Onion Biscuits

These rich, cheesy biscuits are good plain or perfect for the base of a delicious brunch sandwich.

MAKES 1 DOZEN

- Large skillet
- Box-style cheese grater
- Baking sheet, greased, or baking stone

Tips

Make sure all of the ingredients, including your freshly milled flour, are cold before mixing the biscuits together, and chill the cut biscuits in the freezer before baking. Chilling will give you maximum height and flakiness. It's particularly important with this recipe, with the heavier add-ins such as cheese and onions.

If you're using a baking stone, you can chill the cut biscuits on a sheet of parchment paper on a baking sheet. Brush as directed in step 5, then remove from paper and place them directly onto the hot stone without removing it from the oven. Working carefully, simply slide out the oven rack with the stone on it and arrange the biscuits on the hot stone, working quickly, so the oven does not cool down too much. Slide the rack back into the oven and bake as directed.

CARAMELIZED ONIONS

2 tbsp	unsalted butter	28 g
1	large onion, thinly sliced	1

BISCUITS

2½ cups	freshly milled soft wheat flour, chilled after milling	313 g
1 tbsp	honey granules or granulated cane sugar	10 g
2½ tsp	baking powder	12 g
1 tsp	freshly ground black pepper	2 g
½ tsp	salt	3 g
¼ tsp	baking soda	2 g
¾ cup	very cold or frozen unsalted butter	170 g
1 cup	shredded Dubliner (see Tip, page 224) or Gruyère cheese (or your favorite)	114 g
1 cup	cold buttermilk	240 g
1	egg	1
	Freshly ground black pepper	

1. Caramelized Onions: In a large skillet, heat butter over medium-high heat. Add onions and cook, stirring frequently, for about 20 minutes until very soft and golden. Remove from heat and let cool completely.

2. Biscuits: In a large bowl, whisk together flour, honey granules, baking powder, pepper, salt and baking soda. Using the coarse side of a box grater, grate butter directly into flour. Toss to coat. Add Caramelized Onions, cheese and buttermilk and stir with a fork until a shaggy dough forms.

Tip

Turn these into Brunch Biscuits: Cut biscuits in half horizontally. Spread with spicy mustard and layer with slices of roast turkey, a poached egg and arugula.

3. Turn the dough out onto a lightly floured surface. Using your hands, pat into a rectangle, gathering the dough together. Cut into quarters. Stack each quarter on top of each other. Pat down into a rectangle again. Repeat 3 more times. Pat or roll the dough into a rectangle, about 1 inch (2.5 cm) thick. Using a knife, cut into 12 squares, Place biscuits 2 inches (5 cm) apart on prepared pan (see Tip, opposite left). Freeze until cold, about 1 hour, or up to 24 hours.

4. Meanwhile, preheat oven to 425°F (220°C). If using a baking stone, place in oven while preheating.

5. In a small bowl, whisk egg until blended. Brush over tops of biscuits and sprinkle lightly with pepper. Bake in preheated oven for about 15 minutes (adding a few more minutes if baking from frozen) or until golden brown. Serve warm or let cool to room temperature.

SOUPS, STEWS AND CHILIS

Chicken Stock

Chicken (or turkey) meat with bones will give the best flavor but you can make a nice stock with boneless cuts as well.

MAKES ABOUT 9 CUPS (2.12 L)

- Large stock pot or minimum 6-qt (6 L) pressure cooker

2 to 3 lbs	bone-in chicken pieces	908 g to 1.36 kg
3	stalks celery, chopped	3
2 to 3	carrots, chopped	2 to 3
1 to 2	onions, chopped	1 to 2
1	leek, chopped (optional)	1
2 to 3 tsp	whole black peppercorns (or freshly ground pepper to taste)	6 to 9 g
1 tbsp	salt (optional)	18 g
	Cold water	

Tips

Use chicken (or turkey) wing tips, drumsticks or trimmings from breaking down a whole bird into parts or spatchcocking (butterflied). Collect pieces as you prepare various dishes, storing them in the freezer until you have enough for a batch of stock. Drumsticks are a good, economical option if you don't have trimmed pieces.

STOCK YOUR OWN WAY

You can use the quantities of ingredients in these stock recipes as rough guidelines. I vary the amounts of meat, bones, vegetables and seasonings based on what I have on hand. When an ingredient is listed with a range in the quantity (for example, "1 to 2 onions"), the lower amount will give you a milder stock while the higher amount gives a richer, more flavorful stock. You can decide the amount based on the taste you're aiming for or on the ingredients you have on hand.

Remember, recipes are just suggestions, especially when it comes to making your own stocks. Feel free to use what you have on hand and flavors that suit your taste. You can use the scrapings and skins of vegetables used in other recipes that you might typically discard, such as onion skins, the tops of carrots, celery ends or leaves or the darker green ends of leeks.

Stovetop Method

1. In a large stock pot, combine chicken, celery, carrots, onions, leek (if using), peppercorns and salt (if using). Add 11 cups (2.6 L) cold water, or enough to cover bones by about 2 inches (5 cm). Bring to a simmer over high heat. Reduce heat and simmer very gently for about 2 to 2½ hours until stock is flavorful.

2. Strain stock through a sieve into a large bowl or another pot. Discard solids.

3. Use immediately or place bowl or pot into a sink full of ice water to rapidly cool, refreshing ice as necessary, until stock is cold. Skim off fat and discard, if desired. Transfer stock to jars or airtight containers and refrigerate for up to 3 days or freeze for up to 6 months.

Pressure Cooker Method

1. In a pressure cooker, combine chicken, celery, carrots, onions, leek (if using), peppercorns and salt (if using). Add 8 cups (1.89 L) cold water, or enough to cover bones, ensuring you don't exceed maximum fill line in pressure cooker. Lock the pressure lid into place. Heat the pot over high heat and bring pressure to High. Cook for 25 minutes, adjusting heat to maintain pressure as necessary. Remove from heat and let pressure release naturally.

2. Uncover pot. Strain stock through a sieve into a large bowl or another pot. Discard solids.

3. Use immediately or place bowl or pot into a sink full of ice water to rapidly cool, refreshing ice as necessary, until stock is cold. Skim off fat and discard, if desired. Transfer stock to jars or airtight containers and refrigerate for up to 3 days or freeze for up to 6 months.

Variation

Roasted Chicken or Turkey Stock: To use the leftover carcass (or carcasses) from roasted chicken or turkey, just use the amount you have in place of the bone-in chicken pieces. There's no need to weigh them or use a specific quantity.

Beef Stock

Beef stock is not only economical to make but also delicious and nutritious and convenient to have on hand to boost the flavor of your favorite beef soup or stew. I use it in Sue's Chuckwagon Beef Stew and the French Onion Chicken Soup, but I also enjoy it on its own.

MAKES ABOUT 8 CUPS (1.89 L)

- Roasting pan
- Large stock pot or minimum 6-qt (6 L) pressure cooker

Tips

Beef soup bones are available at butcher shops and well-stocked grocery stores (often frozen). You can also use any bone-in cut of beef, such as shank, chuck, oxtail and ribs.

If the bones are completely clean of meat, you can boost the beef flavor by adding trimmings of beef meat along with the bones (save trimmings in the freezer until you're ready to make stock) or add a small amount (about 8 oz / 227 g) of beef stew cubes.

Preheat oven to 400°F (200°C)

2 to 3 lbs	meaty beef soup bones (see Tips, left)	908 g to 1.36 kg
3	stalks celery, chopped	3
2 to 3	carrots, chopped	2 to 3
1 to 2	onions, chopped	1 to 2
1	leek, chopped (optional)	1
2 to 3 tsp	whole black peppercorns (or freshly ground pepper to taste)	6 to 9 g
1 tbsp	salt (optional)	18 g
	Cold water	

SEAR THE BONES

Sometimes I prefer to sear the bones on the stovetop in a wide pot instead of roasting them. I then use the same pot to make my stock so I lose none of the seared meaty flavor. Heat a wide stockpot or an 8-qt (8 L) or larger pressure cooker over medium-high heat, then add about 1 tbsp (14 g) of oil. Add the meaty bones in a single layer, in batches if necessary, to avoid crowding. Sear, turning until well browned on all sides. Add all of the bones back to the pot, if necessary, then proceed with step 2, scraping up the brown bits from the bottom of the pot.

Stovetop Method

1. Place soup bones in roasting pan, spacing them apart. Roast in preheated oven for about 30 minutes or until browned.

2. Transfer bones to a large stock pot; add celery, carrots, onions, leek (if using), peppercorns and salt (if using). Pour 1 cup (250 mL) of water into hot roasting pan and scrape up any brown bits; pour into pot. Add 10 cups (2.36 L) cold water, or enough to cover bones by about 2 inches (5 cm). Bring to a simmer over high heat. Reduce heat and simmer very gently, occasionally skimming any scum that rises to the surface, for 2 to 3 hours, until stock is flavorful.

3. Strain stock through a sieve into a large bowl or another pot. Discard solids.

4. Use immediately or place bowl or pot into a sink full of ice water to rapidly cool, refreshing ice as necessary, until stock is cold. Skim off fat and discard, if desired. Transfer stock to jars or airtight containers and refrigerate for up to 3 days or freeze for up to 6 months.

Pressure Cooker Method

1. Place soup bones in roasting pan, spacing them apart. Roast in preheated oven for about 30 minutes or until browned.

2. Transfer bones to a pressure cooker; add celery, carrots, onions, leek (if using), peppercorns and salt (if using). Pour 1 cup (250 mL) water into hot roasting pan and scrape up any brown bits; pour into pot. Add 7 cups (1.65 L) cold water, or enough to cover bones, ensuring you don't exceed maximum fill line in pressure cooker. Lock the pressure lid into place. Heat the pot over high heat and bring pressure to High. Cook for 25 minutes, adjusting heat to maintain pressure as necessary. Remove from heat and let pressure release naturally.

3. Uncover pot. Strain stock through a sieve into a large bowl or another pot. Discard solids.

4. Use immediately or place bowl or pot into a sink full of ice water to rapidly cool, refreshing ice as necessary, until stock is cold. Skim off fat and discard, if desired. Transfer stock to jars or airtight containers and refrigerate for up to 3 days or freeze for up to 6 months.

Vegetable Stock

This delicious vegetable broth works well as a base for vegetarian and vegan soups and stews and as a cooking liquid for rice. You can replace a beef or chicken stock or broth in any recipe with vegetable stock or broth, although the flavor of the soup will be lighter. You can include other vegetable scraps (collected in the fridge or freezer) and herb stems in addition to the vegetables called for in this recipe.

MAKES ABOUT 8 CUPS (1.89 L)

- Large stock pot or minimum 6-qt (6 L) pressure cooker

Tips

You don't need to peel the potatoes or carrots when making stock but do give them a good scrub with a brush under running water before chopping.

2 to 3	potatoes, chopped	2 to 3
2 to 3	stalks celery, chopped	2 to 3
2 to 3	carrots, chopped	2 to 3
1 to 2	onions, chopped	1 to 2
1	leek, chopped (optional)	1
2 to 3 tsp	whole black peppercorns (or freshly ground pepper to taste)	6 to 9 g
1 tbsp	salt (optional)	18 g
	Bay leaf (optional)	
	Sprigs of fresh thyme (optional)	
	Cold water	

EASY TOMATO SOUP

After making this vegetable stock, you can repurpose some of the vegetables into an easy tomato soup. At the end of step 2, save the potatoes, celery, carrots and as much of the onions and leeks as desired. Add the reserved vegetables to 4 to 6 cups (944 mL to 1.42 L) of vegetable stock in a pot; bring to a simmer over medium heat. Purée with an immersion blender in the pot (or transfer to a blender in batches). Stir in a jar (about 24 oz / 690 g) of passata* (strained tomatoes) and season with salt and pepper to taste. Heat until steaming. If desired, stir in heavy or whipping (35%) cream to taste for cream of tomato soup.

*Passata is a popular uncooked tomato purée product commonly used in Italian cooking and may be labeled as "strained tomatoes." You can find it in most grocery stores in the canned vegetable or pasta section or with the international foods.

Stovetop Method

1. In a large stock pot, combine potatoes, celery, carrots, onions, leek (if using) and peppercorns; add salt, bay leaf and thyme (if using). Add 10 cups (2.36 L) cold water, or enough to cover vegetables by about 2 inches (5 cm). Bring to a simmer over high heat. Reduce heat and simmer very gently for 30 to 45 minutes, until stock is flavorful.

2. Strain stock through a sieve into a large bowl or another pot. Discard solids.

3. Use immediately or place bowl or pot into a sink full of ice water to rapidly cool, refreshing ice as necessary, until stock is cold. Transfer to jars or airtight containers and refrigerate for up to 3 days or freeze for up to 6 months.

Pressure Cooker Method

1. In a pressure cooker, combine potatoes, celery, carrots, onions, leek and peppercorns; add salt, bay leaf and thyme (if using). Add 8 cups (1.89 L) cold water, or enough to cover vegetables, ensuring you don't exceed maximum fill line in pressure cooker. Lock the pressure lid into place. Heat the pot over high heat and bring pressure to High. Cook for 20 minutes, adjusting heat to maintain pressure as necessary. Remove from heat and let pressure release naturally.

2. Uncover pot. Strain stock through a sieve into a large bowl or another pot. Discard solids.

3. Use immediately or place bowl or pot into a sink full of ice water to rapidly cool, refreshing ice as necessary, until stock is cold. Transfer to jars or airtight containers and refrigerate for up to 3 days or freeze for up to 6 months.

Variation

Mushroom Stock: Omit the potatoes and add about 1½ lbs (681 g) of mushrooms, using at least two varieties; add 1 tbsp (15 g) tamari sauce and 4 chopped cloves garlic with vegetables. Simmer for 30 minutes (when simmered longer, the broth might become bitter), then strain as directed.

3-Minute Instant "Cream of" Soup Base

I learned how to make this healthy substitute for cream of chicken soup to replace the not-so-healthy canned versions so often used in some favorite casserole and other dishes. This recipe makes enough to replace one 10 oz (284 g) can of soup. It is completely dairy free, ready in minutes and versatile. You can make it whatever flavor you want it to be and serve it as a stand-alone soup.

MAKES $1\frac{3}{4}$ CUPS (425 G)

- Small saucepan

Tips

Any type of stock or broth may be used for this soup. For cream of chicken, use chicken stock or broth. You can also use beef or mushroom stock or broth. If mushroom is not available, add ¼ cup (19 g) diced mushrooms to beef or vegetable stock or broth to create a cream of mushroom soup base.

The amount of flour used will determine how thick the soup is. You want it thick for a canned soup substitute in a recipe. But if you want a thinner soup for eating, start by whisking in about 2 tbsp (14 g) of the flour adding a little more at a time until the desired thickness is achieved.

2 cups	stock or broth (see Tip, left)	472 g
⅓ cup	freshly milled bean or legume flour	38 g

1. In a small saucepan, bring broth to a boil over high heat. Whisk in flour; immediately reduce heat and simmer, whisking constantly, for about 3 minutes until thickened. Remove from heat. Use immediately or let cool completely. (The base thickens considerably as it cools.) Store in a jar or airtight container for up to 3 days.

BEAN OR LEGUME FLOUR

Any type of bean or legume flour may be used. For a mild flavor replacement for cream of chicken soup, use a white bean flour, such as Great Northern, navy, garbanzo (chickpea) or baby lima bean flour. For darker broths, like beef or mushroom, you can use a darker, more flavorful flour such as black-eyed pea or pinto bean flour. You can also change up the flavor of your soup by using different legume flours such as lentils or split peas.

Chicken Soup Base

You'll get the most flavorful soups and stocks when you make them in a pressure cooker, though you can come very close to the best in a large pot on the stove. To save time, start the chicken and water heating in the pot while you chop the vegetables. This is my chicken soup base for any number of variations of chicken soup. Whether it's Classic Chicken Noodle, Classic Chicken and Brown Rice or Whole Grains (page 97) or Make It Chicken and Dumplings (page 98), this is your starting point.

MAKES 6 TO 8 SERVINGS

- Large pot or minimum 6-qt (6 L) pressure cooker

Tips

Always start with cold water, not hot water. Cold water draws the most flavor out of the meat you are cooking.

Bone-in chicken will give the most flavor, but when in a hurry I have used 2 lbs (908 g) boneless skinless chicken breast, thighs or a combination of the two in place of the whole chicken. Using boneless chicken eliminates time spent waiting for the chicken to cool before you can shred and add it back to the pot, allowing you to have delicious chicken soup ready to eat in less than 30 minutes.

If making this soup base ahead (see page 31), reheat until steaming and then proceed with the variation add-ins as desired.

1	whole chicken (3½ to 5 lbs / 1.59 to 2.27 kg)	1
6 cups	cold water (approx.)	1.42 L
3	stalks celery, diced	3
1	onion, chopped	1
1½ cups	diced carrots	192 g
1 tbsp	salt	18 g
1 to 2 tbsp	dried Italian seasoning	3 to 6 g
	Freshly ground black pepper	

Stovetop Method

1. Place chicken breast-side down in a large pot. Add 6 cups (1.42 L) water and heat on high. Add celery, onion, carrots, salt, Italian seasoning and pepper to taste. Add more water to cover, if necessary. Bring to a boil.

2. Cover and reduce heat to low and simmer for 1 to 2 hours until chicken is tender and beginning to pull away from the bone.

3. Using tongs, transfer chicken from pot to a large bowl, leaving stock and vegetables in pot. Let chicken cool enough to handle. Remove skin and meat from bones; discard skin and bones. All or part of the meat may be chopped or torn into bite-size pieces and added back to the soup as desired or reserved for another use.

Bread Pairing

Roasted Carrot Sage Biscuits (page 84)

Pressure Cooker Method

1. Place chicken breast-side down in a pressure cooker. Add 6 cups (1.42 L) cold water and heat on high. Add celery, onion, carrots, salt, Italian seasoning and pepper to taste. Add more water to cover if necessary, ensuring you don't exceed maximum fill line in pressure cooker.

2. Lock the pressure lid into place. Heat the pot over high heat and bring pressure to High. Cook for 18 minutes for a 3½-lb (1.59 kg) chicken, adding 5 minutes cooking time for each additional pound (454 g), adjusting heat to maintain pressure as necessary. Remove from heat and let pressure release naturally. The chicken should be tender and beginning to pull away from the bone. If not, return to pressure and continue to cook in 5-minute increments until chicken is tender.

3. Uncover pot. Using tongs, transfer chicken from pot to a large bowl, leaving stock and vegetables in pot. Let chicken cool enough to handle. Remove skin and meat from bones; discard skin and bones. All or part of the meat may be chopped or torn into bite-size pieces and added back to the soup as desired or reserved for another use.

Variations

Classic Chicken Noodle Soup: At the end of step 3, add desired amount of chicken to soup. Return to a boil over high heat. Add 1 cup (125 g) whole-grain elbow macaroni or 1½ cups (128 g) whole-grain rotini or fusilli pasta and boil according to package directions (usually about 5 to 8 minutes), stirring occasionally, until pasta is tender.

Classic Chicken and Brown Rice Soup (Stovetop Method): In a medium saucepan, combine 1 tbsp (14 g) olive oil, 1 cup (200 g) whole-grain brown rice and ½ tsp (3 g) salt. Cook over medium heat, stirring, for 2 to 3 minutes until rice is slightly toasted and fragrant. Stir in 2 cups (472 g) water; bring to a boil. Cover, reduce heat to low and simmer, stirring occasionally, for 45 minutes to 1 hour or according to package directions, until rice is tender and liquid is absorbed. Remove from heat and let stand, covered, for 5 to 10 minutes. Stir into soup with chopped chicken in step 3.

Classic Chicken and Brown Rice Soup (Pressure Cooker Method): In a medium (minimum 3½ qt / 3.5 L) pressure cooker, combine 1 tbsp (14 g) olive oil, 1 cup (200 g) whole-grain brown rice and ½ tsp (3 g) salt. Cook over medium heat, stirring, for 2 to 3 minutes until rice is slightly toasted and fragrant. Stir in 2 cups (472 g) water; increase heat to high and bring to a boil. Stir once. Lock the pressure lid into place. Heat the pot over high heat and bring pressure to High. Cook for 18 minutes, adjusting heat as necessary to maintain pressure. Remove from heat and let pressure release naturally. The rice should be tender and liquid absorbed; if not, return to pressure and cook in 2-minute increments until tender. Stir into soup with chopped chicken in step 3.

Classic Chicken Soup with Whole Grains (Stovetop Method): Add 1 cup (210 g) whole-grain Kamut or 1 cup (180 g) hulled whole barley with the vegetables in step 1. Cook as directed.

Classic Chicken Soup with Whole Grains (Pressure Cooker Method): Add 1 cup (210 g) whole-grain Kamut or 1 cup (180 g) hulled whole barley to the pot in step 1 with the vegetables. Cook as directed.

Make It Chicken and Dumplings

It is so easy to turn your Chicken Soup Base into Chicken and Dumplings. No need for a special recipe! I like to add a little yogurt or sour cream to the soup to give it the desired creaminess, then use either a biscuit-style dumpling or noodle-style dumpling to create the perfect comforting soup. This was one of my kids' favorites, especially the noodle style, which they lovingly nicknamed chicken and slabs.

MAKES 6 TO 8 SERVINGS

Tips

I usually include the yogurt or sour cream to make this a creamy soup, though it is optional if you prefer a clear broth as shown in the photo.

Instead of cutting cold butter into the flour mixture, you can use melted butter and add it with the milk.

1	recipe Chicken Soup Base (page 95)	1
1 cup	full-fat yogurt or sour cream, optional (see Tip, left)	240 g

BISCUIT-STYLE DUMPLINGS

2½ cups	freshly milled soft wheat flour	313 g
2 tsp	baking powder	10 g
¾ tsp	salt	5 g
½ tsp	baking soda	3 g
⅓ cup	cold unsalted butter	76 g
2 tbsp	dried Italian seasoning or favorite herbs	6 g
¾ cup to 1 cup	whole milk	180 to 240 g

1. Prepare Chicken Soup Base as directed through step 3; keep warm.

2. Biscuit-Style Dumplings: In a medium bowl, combine flour, baking powder, salt and baking soda. Using a pastry blender or two knives, cut in butter until crumbly. Add $\frac{3}{4}$ cup (180 g) of the milk; stir just to combine (the dough should be fairly loose but not runny). If it's too dry, add a bit more milk, 1 to 2 tbsp (15 to 30 g) at a time, stirring just until incorporated. Do not overmix dough. Let stand for a few minutes until dough has stiffened slightly.

3. If using, in a small bowl, combine yogurt with about 1 cup (240 g) of broth from the soup; whisk until smooth.

4. Bring remaining soup to a simmer over medium heat. Add yogurt mixture, stirring to fully incorporate. Reduce heat to maintain a gentle but steady simmer. Using a small scoop or tablespoon, drop dumplings into simmering soup around the edges of the pot, working in a circle. Using the back of a spoon, gently press the dumpling down to allow the broth to run over the tops of the dumplings.

5. Cover the pot with a lid, leaving lid slightly ajar. Simmer for about 15 to 20 minutes, gently stirring once while cooking and using the back of a large spoon to press the dumplings into broth again, until dumplings are cooked through. To check for doneness, using a slotted spoon, remove one dumpling from the soup and cut it in half to check that the inside is no longer wet. If not done, cover and cook about 3 to 4 minutes longer.

6. Ladle soup into bowls with 2 or 3 dumplings in each serving.

Variation

Noodle-Style Dumplings: In a medium bowl, combine 2 cups (250 g) freshly milled soft wheat flour, 4 tsp (20 g) baking powder and $\frac{3}{4}$ tsp (4 g) salt. Using a pastry blender or two knives, cut in 2 tbsp (28 g) unsalted butter until crumbly. Add $\frac{2}{3}$ cup (160 g) whole milk and stir until a soft ball of dough forms. On a floured surface, roll dough very thinly, to about $\frac{1}{8}$-inch (3 mm) thickness. Cut into strips, each about $1\frac{1}{2}$ inches (4 cm) long and about $\frac{3}{4}$ inch (2 cm) wide. Drop into soup as directed in step 4, but without pressing to immerse in broth. Cover pot with lid and simmer about 20 minutes until noodles are tender, gently stirring once halfway through cooking.

Make It Chicken and Dumplings
(page 98)

Chicken Pot Pie Soup

Imagine all the flavors and comfort you love but served as a soup instead of a pot pie. This is it — creamy, hearty and delicious. I love most any type of pie but the crust is always my favorite part. It's so easy to just roll out the dough and bake it on a baking sheet. Cut in strips or broken into pieces, this addition gives you the goodness of a pot pie without all the fuss.

MAKES 6 SERVINGS

- Large pot or minimum 6-qt (6 L) pressure cooker
- Medium saucepan
- Baking sheet or baking stone

Tip

I have learned to use a mild bean flour instead of wheat flour to thicken many of my soups and meat gravy. No need to make a roux or slurry to keep it from clumping; simply whisk the bean flour directly into the simmering broth. Flour made from white beans such as garbanzo (chickpea), Great Northern or baby limas is mild in flavor and won't alter the taste of your soup or gravy.

1½ lbs	boneless skinless chicken breasts, cut into ½-inch (1 cm) pieces	681 g
6 cups	cold water	1.42 L
3	medium russet or yellow-flesh potatoes (peeled if desired), diced	3
2	stalks celery, diced	2
1	small onion, diced	1
1 cup	diced carrots	128 g
2 tsp	dried Italian seasoning	2 g
	Salt and freshly ground black pepper	
2 cups	chicken stock or broth	472 g
⅓ cup	white bean flour	38 g
Half	recipe Perfect Pie Dough (page 106), chilled	Half
10 oz	frozen green peas (optional)	284 g

Stovetop Method

1. In a large pot, combine chicken, cold water, potatoes, celery, onion and carrots. Add Italian seasoning, 1 tbsp (18 g) salt, and 1 tsp (2 g) pepper. Bring to a boil over high heat. Cover, reduce heat to low and simmer, stirring occasionally, for about 20 minutes or until chicken is no longer pink inside and vegetables are tender.

2. Meanwhile, in a medium saucepan, bring the stock to a boil over high heat. Reduce heat to low and whisk in bean flour. Simmer, whisking, for 2 to 3 minutes, until thickened. Set aside.

3. Preheat oven to 425°F (220°C) with baking stone on middle rack, if using.

4. On a floured surface, roll out pie dough into a rough circle until ¼ inch (5 mm) thick. Sprinkle lightly with salt and pepper, if desired. Transfer to a baking sheet or preheated baking stone. Bake in preheated oven for 10 minutes until puffed and golden brown. Let cool slightly on a wire rack. Cut into ¾-inch (2 cm) wide strips, about 2 inches (5 cm) long, or break into pieces; set aside.

5. Uncover the soup pot. Return soup to a simmer over low heat. Whisk in thickened stock mixture; stir in peas (if using). Simmer, uncovered, stirring occasionally, for 5 to 10 minutes, until peas are hot, soup is thickened and flavors are blended.

6. Ladle hot soup into serving bowls and top with the pie-crust pieces.

Pressure Cooker Method

1. In a pressure cooker, combine chicken, cold water, potatoes, celery, onion and carrots. Add Italian seasoning, 1 tbsp (18 g) salt, and 1 tsp (2 g) pepper. Lock the pressure lid into place. Heat the pot over high heat and bring pressure to High. Cook for 5 minutes, adjusting heat to maintain pressure as necessary. Remove from heat and let pressure release naturally. The chicken should no longer be pink inside and the vegetables should be tender. If not, return to pressure and cook in 2-minute increments until done.

2. Meanwhile, in a medium saucepan, bring the stock to a boil over high heat. Reduce heat to low and whisk in bean flour. Simmer, whisking, for 2 to 3 minutes, until thickened. Set aside.

3. Preheat oven to 425°F (220°C) with baking stone on middle rack, if using.

4. On a floured surface, roll out pie dough in a rough circle until ¼ inch (5 mm) thick. Sprinkle lightly with salt and pepper, if desired. Transfer to a baking sheet or preheated baking stone. Bake in preheated oven for 10 minutes until puffed and golden brown. Let cool slightly on a wire rack. Cut into ¾-inch (2 cm) wide strips, about 2 inches (5 cm) long, or break into pieces; set aside.

5. Uncover pressure cooker. Return soup to a simmer over low heat. Whisk in thickened stock mixture; stir in peas (if using). Simmer, uncovered, stirring occasionally, for 5 to 10 minutes, until peas are hot, soup is thickened and flavors are blended.

6. Ladle hot soup into serving bowls and top with the pie-crust pieces.

Chicken Pot Pie Soup (page 102)
and Perfect Pie Dough (page 106)

Perfect Pie Dough

This is my favorite flaky pie dough recipe. I have included all the basic instructions for a traditional double, single and prebaked pie crust. For the Chicken Pot Pie Soup, simply prepare the dough as directed, roll it out and bake on a baking sheet. When making pie dough it is important that all ingredients are chilled. Freshly milled flour will be warm, so to ensure a flaky baked pastry, place it in the refrigerator or freezer to cool before cutting in the cold butter.

MAKES TWO 9-INCH (23 CM) PIE CRUSTS

- Pastry blender
- Rolling pin
- One or two 9-inch (23 cm) pie plates (optional)

2¾ cups	freshly milled soft wheat flour, chilled	344 g
1 tsp	salt	6 g
1 cup	cold unsalted butter, divided	227 g
⅓ cup	cold water, divided (approx.)	79 g
	Additional freshly milled soft wheat flour (for rolling)	

1. In a large bowl, combine the flour and salt. Cut three-quarters of the cold butter into small cubes. Using a pastry blender, cut cubed butter into the flour until the mixture looks like coarse cornmeal. Rub the butter and flour together between your hands and palms until the flour takes on a creamy yellow color. Be thorough — you can't overwork the dough at this point.

2. Cut the remaining butter into small pieces. Using a pastry blender, cut these pieces into the mixture as before but leaving the chunks of butter pea-sized. These larger chunks will create steam during baking and add to the flakiness of the final pie crust.

3. Make a well in the center of the mixture. Add ⅓ cup (79 g) cold water. Using a fork, blend the water into the flour mixture. The mixture will still be crumbly, but it should look moist. If it looks too dry, add an additional 1 to 2 tbsp (15 to 30 g) cold water, as necessary, until mixture is moistened but still crumbly.

4. Turn the mixture out onto a clean work surface and form it into a mound. Knead lightly, just until the dough loses its dry, crumbly appearance. Gather it into a ball, pressing it firmly so it holds together. Cut the dough into two equal portions. Shape each into a disk and wrap with plastic wrap. Chill for at least 1 hour before rolling. (Dough may be chilled like this for up to 5 days.)

5. Remove from refrigerator and roll as desired on a floured surface. Flour is your friend in this step. Roll, rotating the dough, until it is about $\frac{1}{8}$ inch (3 mm) thick and about 1 inch (2.5 cm) larger than the pie plate you are using. Brush away excess flour and gently transfer to pie plate, making sure not to stretch the dough. Trim the edge of the dough, leaving about $\frac{1}{2}$ inch (1 cm) over the edge of the pie plate for a single-crust pie. (See instructions below for a Double-Crust Filled Pie.) Turn the extra dough under to make a neat, thickened border. Flute as desired.

For Single-Crust Prebaked Pie Crust

6. Prick the dough all over with the tines of a fork to prevent bubbles from forming in the crust while baking. Refrigerate or freeze the shaped pie shell for at least 20 minutes before baking.

7. Meanwhile, preheat oven to 375°F (190°C).

8. Line the chilled crust with parchment paper, pressing it firmly up against the bottom and sides. Fill parchment paper with dried beans or pie weights.

9. Bake for 25 minutes or until the edge begins to color. Remove the parchment and beans. Return to oven and bake for 5 minutes for a partially baked crust or 12 to 15 minutes for a fully baked crust. Let cool, as directed in your recipe.

For Double-Crust Filled Pie

6. Preheat oven according to your pie recipe.

7. Roll out bottom crust as described above in step 5 and trim, leaving 1 inch (2.5 cm) over the edge of the pie plate. Spread filling into crust. Brush the edge of the bottom crust with water.

8. Roll out the top crust to slightly larger than your pie plate, so that it will adequately cover the filling. Place the top crust over the filling as evenly as possible. Trim the crust leaving a 1-inch (2.5 cm) border. Fold bottom and top edges under together, seal and flute or decorate, as desired. Cut at least 4 vents in the top of the crust at even intervals to allow steam to escape as the pie bakes. Bake as directed in your recipe.

Lemon Chicken and Barley Soup

This light soup with a pleasant lemon flavor is perfect for when you want a less heavy meal. The traditional recipe uses pastina (a small round pasta), but I replaced the pasta with hulled barley for a nice whole-grain touch of fiber and flavor. It's delicious served with one of the suggested breads and tzatziki.

MAKES 6 TO 8 SERVINGS

- Large pot or minimum 6-qt (6 L) pressure cooker

1/4 cup	extra virgin olive oil	57 g
1	small onion, finely chopped	1
	Salt and freshly ground black pepper	
1	whole chicken (2 to 3 lbs / 908 g to 1.36 kg)	1
4 cups	cold water	944 mL
4 cups	chicken stock or broth	944 mL
	Juice of 2 lemons, divided	
1/2 cup	hulled barley	90 g
2	large eggs	2
2	large egg yolks	2
2 cups	packed fresh spinach, stems removed	60 g
1/4 cup	chopped fresh dill	12 g
	Crumbled feta cheese (optional)	

Bread Pairing

Authentic Pan Pita (page 65) or
Indian Naan (page 66)

Stovetop Method

1. In a large pot, heat oil over high heat. Add onion, 2 tsp (12 g) salt and pepper to taste; cook, stirring, for about 3 minutes or until softened. Add chicken, cold water, stock and juice of 1 lemon. Bring to a boil over high heat. Cover, reduce heat and simmer for 30 minutes. Add barley, cover and simmer for about 1 hour or until chicken is beginning to pull away from the bone and barley is tender.

2. Uncover pot. Using tongs, transfer chicken from pot to a large bowl, leaving soup and vegetables in pot. Cover pot and keep soup hot. Let chicken cool enough to handle. Remove skin and meat from bones; discard skin and bones. Shred meat into bite-size pieces; set aside.

3. In a medium bowl, whisk remaining lemon juice into eggs and egg yolks until frothy. Gradually whisk a ladleful of the hot soup into the egg mixture. Then gradually pour the egg mixture into the soup while whisking. Cook over medium-low heat, stirring, for about 1 minute, until slightly thickened and creamy.

4. Reduce heat to low and stir in shredded chicken, spinach and dill. Season with salt and pepper to taste.

5. Ladle soup into bowls and top with crumbled feta, if desired.

Pressure Cooker Method

1. In a pressure cooker, heat oil over high heat. Add onion, 2 tsp (12 g) salt and pepper to taste; cook, stirring, for about 3 minutes or until softened. Add chicken, cold water, stock, juice of 1 lemon and barley. Lock the pressure lid into place. Heat the pot over high heat and bring pressure to High. Cook for 15 minutes, adjusting heat as necessary to maintain pressure. Remove from heat and let pressure release naturally. The chicken should be beginning to pull away from the bone and the barley should be tender. If not, return to pressure and cook in 5-minute increments until done.

2. Uncover pot. Using tongs, transfer chicken from pot to a large bowl, leaving soup and vegetables in pot. Cover pot and keep soup hot. Let chicken cool enough to handle. Remove skin and meat from bones; discard skin and bones. Shred meat into bite-size pieces; set aside.

3. In a medium bowl, whisk remaining lemon juice into eggs and egg yolks until frothy. Gradually whisk a ladleful of the hot soup into the egg mixture. Then gradually pour the egg mixture into the soup while whisking. Cook over medium-low heat, stirring, for about 1 minute, until slightly thickened and creamy.

4. Reduce heat to low and stir in shredded chicken, spinach and dill. Season with salt and pepper to taste.

5. Ladle soup into bowls and top with crumbled feta, if desired.

Lemon Chicken and Barley Soup (page 108) and Authentic Pan Pita (page 65)

Tex-Mex Chicken Soup

Serve this warming soup with corn chips and Brad's Incredible Salsa (page 187) and a slice of bread or a muffin and you have a delicious and satisfying meal.

MAKES 8 SERVINGS

- Large pot or minimum 6-qt (6 L) pressure cooker

Tips

Canned beans can be used to save prep time instead of cooking from dry. Use one 14- to 15-oz (398 to 425 g) can black beans and three 14- to 15-oz (398 to 425 g) cans of Great Northern beans (or navy beans). Use the liquid in the beans to add a nice, thick texture to the soup (no need to drain or rinse).

For this recipe I like to include the liquid from cooking beans from dried in a pressure cooker. To measure the black beans with liquid, scoop the beans out of the pot with a slotted spoon and measure 1½ cups (270 g), then measure ⅔ cup (155 g) liquid and add both to the soup. For the Great Northern beans, measure 4½ cups (810 g) beans and 2¼ cups (540 g) liquid.

3 tbsp	olive oil	42 g
1	onion, diced	1
2 to 3 tbsp	adobo seasoning (see Tip, page 128), divided	36 to 54 g
2 tsp	ground cumin, divided	4 g
3 or 4	boneless skinless chicken breasts, cut into bite-size pieces	3 or 4
6 cups	chicken stock or broth	1.42 L
1 tsp	salt	6 g
½ tsp	seasoning salt	3 g
1	can (4 oz / 113 g) chopped green chilies	1
1¾ cups	cooked black beans with liquid (see page 29 and Tip, left)	425 g
4½ cups	cooked Great Northern beans with liquid (see page 29 and Tip, left)	1.35 kg
1	can (15 oz / 425 g) whole kernel corn (optional)	
1 cup	heavy or whipping (35%) cream	240 g

Stovetop Method

1. In a large pot, heat oil over medium-high heat. Add onion, 2 tbsp (36 g) of the adobo seasoning, 1 tsp (2 g) of the cumin and chicken. Cook, stirring constantly, for about 5 minutes or until onions are translucent. Add stock, salt and seasoning salt; bring to a boil. Reduce heat and simmer, stirring occasionally, for 15 to 20 minutes, until the chicken is no longer pink inside.

2. Return soup to medium-high heat. Add green chilies, black beans, Great Northern beans and corn (if using). Season with more of the remaining adobo seasoning and cumin to taste, if desired. Bring to a boil. Reduce heat and simmer, uncovered, stirring occasionally, for about 5 minutes or until heated through and flavors are blended. Stir in cream and simmer, stirring occasionally, for about 5 more minutes, until soup is slightly thickened.

3. Ladle soup into bowls.

Pressure Cooker Method

1. In a pressure cooker, heat oil over medium-high heat. Add onion, 2 tbsp (36 g) of the adobo seasoning, 1 tsp (2 g) of the cumin and chicken. Cook, stirring constantly, for about 5 minutes or until onions are translucent. Add stock, salt and seasoning salt. Lock the pressure lid into place. Heat the pot over high heat and bring pressure to High. Cook for 5 minutes, adjusting heat as necessary to maintain pressure. Remove from heat and quick-release the pressure or let pressure release naturally.

2. Uncover pot. Return soup to medium-high heat. Add green chilies, black beans, Great Northern beans and corn (if using). Season with more of the remaining adobo seasoning and cumin to taste, if desired. Bring to a boil. Reduce heat and simmer, uncovered, stirring occasionally, for about 5 minutes or until heated through and flavors are blended. Stir in cream and simmer for about 5 more minutes, until soup is slightly thickened.

3. Ladle soup into bowls.

Bread Pairing

Cheddar-Jalapeño Bread (page 37) or
Cheddar Corn Jalapeño Muffins (page 75)

Tex-Mex Chicken Soup (page 112) and
Cheddar Corn Jalapeño Muffins (page 75)

Thai-Style Chicken and Mushroom Noodle Soup

Try this unique and flavorful twist on chicken noodle soup. The prepared dried mushroom seasoning powder (see Tip) gives it an unmistakable umami flavor, taking chicken noodle soup to another level with savory goodness! Multiply the mushroomy goodness by serving with a slice of delicious Mushroom Cheese Bread.

MAKES 6 SERVINGS

- Medium pot

Tips

If fresh lemongrass is not available, look for lemongrass purée in tubes, often shelved in the produce section with fresh herbs at well-stocked supermarkets. Use 1 tbsp (15 g) purée and add it in step 2 (skipping step 1).

There are several brands of dried mushroom seasoning powder available to choose from. Look for one that has dried mushroom powder, garlic and salt as the key ingredients. Or you can substitute 1 clove of minced garlic and another herb seasoning blend or umami seasoning, if you prefer.

For the noodles, I use whole-grain Kamut fettuccini; you can use which ever type of noodles you prefer.

1	stalk lemongrass	1
1	1-inch (2.5 cm) piece fresh gingerroot, peeled and minced	1
1	can (14 oz / 398 mL) coconut milk	1
6 cups	chicken stock or broth	1.42 L
1	boneless skinless chicken breast	1
1 tbsp	dried mushroom seasoning powder	8 g
2 tsp	salt	6 g
	Grated zest of 1 lime	
	Juice of $\frac{1}{2}$ a lime	
1 cup	trimmed mushrooms, chopped (preferably shiitake)	75 g
8 oz	thin rice or whole-grain noodles (see Tip, left)	227 g
$\frac{1}{4}$ cup	cherry tomatoes, chopped	38 g
	Fresh cilantro, chopped	
1	lime, cut into wedges	1
1	jalapeño pepper, seeded and sliced	1

Stovetop Method

1. Cut lemongrass into 3-inch (8 cm) long pieces; smash with the broad side of a knife to release the aromas.

2. In a medium pot, combine lemongrass, ginger, coconut milk and stock. Bring to a simmer over medium heat. Cover, reduce heat to low and simmer for about 30 minutes to infuse the broth.

3. Meanwhile, cut the chicken into $\frac{1}{4}$- to $\frac{1}{2}$-inch (5 mm to 1 cm) pieces and place in a bowl. Add mushroom seasoning powder, salt, lime zest and lime juice; toss to coat.

4. Remove the lemongrass pieces from broth; discard. Stir chicken and chopped mushrooms into broth. Bring to a simmer over medium heat. Simmer, uncovered, stirring occasionally, for about 15 minutes or until chicken is no longer pink inside.

5. Increase heat to medium-high and bring broth to a vigorous simmer. Break up the noodles and stir into soup. Cook for about 3 to 4 minutes or according to the package directions, until noodles are tender.

6. Ladle soup into bowls. Garnish with tomatoes, cilantro, a wedge of lime and jalapeño slices.

Bread Pairing

Mushroom Cheese Bread (page 44)

Thai-Style Chicken and Mushroom Noodle Soup (page 116)
and Mushroom Cheese Bread (page 44)

Cock-a-Leekie Soup

This porridge-like soup is one of the oldest and best-known Scottish dishes. The first known printed recipe appeared in 1598. The name comes from the traditional ingredients of chicken (cock) and leeks (leekie). White wine and vegetables add flavor and barley adds texture, making the soup more filling and warming — perfect for a cold, damp winter day. Traditionally prunes are included to add a balance of sweetness to the flavor, but they can be omitted, as in this recipe, for those who don't like to mix their sweet and savory. To get the full flavor, add a slice of Prune-Feta-Rosemary Crusty No-Knead Bread. I put the prunes in the bread instead of the soup!

MAKES ABOUT 6 TO 8 SERVINGS

- Medium saucepan or medium (minimum 3½-qt / 3.5 L) pressure cooker
- Large pot or minimum 6-qt (6 L) pressure cooker

Tips

The metric weights have been calculated as precise conversions from imperial volumes. For ease, you can round the quantities up or down slightly in this soup and still get good results.

If making the soup ahead, you may want to add the cooked barley when ready to serve, as it will absorb some of the broth, causing the soup to thicken.

When reheating leftovers, some chicken stock or broth may need to be added to thin the soup.

½ cup	hulled barley	90 g
1 cup	water	236 g
2 tbsp	oil	28 g
4 cups	sliced leeks (white and light green parts only, in half-moon slices)	360 g
1 cup	sliced carrots	128 g
4 to 6	cloves garlic, minced	4 to 6
2	bone-in chicken breasts	2
6 cups	cold water	1.42 L
1 cup	dry white wine	236 g
1½ cups	diced potatoes	195 g
1	bay leaf	1
1 tsp	grated lemon zest (about half a lemon)	2 g
	Salt	
1 tbsp	fresh lemon juice	15 g
½ tsp	freshly ground black pepper	1 g
	Chopped fresh parsley (optional)	

Stovetop Method

1. In a medium saucepan, combine barley and 1 cup (236 g) water. Bring to a boil over high heat. Cover, reduce heat to low and simmer for about 1 hour until barley is tender and liquid is absorbed. Set aside.

2. Meanwhile, in a large pot, heat oil over high heat. Add leeks, carrots and garlic. Cook, stirring, for 2 to 3 minutes or until vegetables are tender. Add chicken, cold water, wine, potatoes, bay leaf, lemon zest and 1 tbsp (18 g) salt. Bring to a boil. Reduce heat and simmer, stirring occasionally, for 20 to 30 minutes or until an instant-read thermometer inserted into thickest part of chicken registers 165°F (74°C). Remove from heat.

3. Using tongs, remove chicken from soup to a plate. Let cool slightly. Remove skin, if necessary, and meat from bones; discard skin and bones. Chop or tear meat into bite-size pieces; return to soup. Stir in lemon juice and pepper; season with salt to taste. Stir in cooked barley.

4. Ladle into bowls and garnish with fresh parsley, if desired.

Pressure Cooker Method

1. In a medium pressure cooker, combine barley and 1 cup (236 g) water. Lock the pressure lid into place. Heat the pot over high heat and bring pressure to High. Cook for 18 minutes, adjusting heat as necessary to maintain pressure. Remove from heat and let pressure release naturally. The barley should be tender. If not, return to pressure and cook in 2-minute increments until done. Set aside.

2. Meanwhile, in a large pressure cooker, heat oil over high heat. Add leeks, carrots and garlic. Cook, stirring, for 2 to 3 minutes or until vegetables are tender. Add chicken, cold water, wine, potatoes, bay leaf, lemon zest and 1 tbsp (18 g) salt. Lock pressure lid into place. Heat the pot over high heat and bring pressure to High. Cook for 10 minutes, adjusting heat as necessary to maintain pressure. Let pressure release naturally. Test the chicken to ensure an instant-read thermometer inserted into thickest part of chicken registers 165°F (74°C). If not, return to pressure and cook in 2-minute increments until done.

3. Uncover soup pot. Using tongs, remove chicken from soup to a plate. Let cool slightly. Remove skin, if necessary, and meat from bones; discard skin and bones. Chop or tear meat into bite-size pieces; return to soup. Stir in lemon juice and pepper; season with salt to taste. Stir in cooked barley.

4. Ladle into bowls and garnish with fresh parsley, if desired.

Bread Pairing

Prune-Feta-Rosemary Crusty No-Knead Bread (page 51)

Cock-a-Leekie Soup (page 120) and
Prune-Feta-Rosemary Crusty No-Knead Bread (page 51)

Chicken and Wild Rice Soup (page 124) and
Dubliner Cheese and Caramelized Onion Biscuits (page 82)

Creamy Adobo Chicken Soup

This zesty and robust Creamy Adobo Chicken Soup is a one-pot wonder. The tortilla chips cooked right in the soup along with the added milk and cheese thicken it up nicely. Top with fresh cilantro, avocado and a slice of lime and enjoy.

MAKES 6 SERVINGS

- Large pot or minimum 6-qt (6 L) pressure cooker

Tip

Adobo seasoning, a dried herb and spice blend, is available in the spice section of well-stocked supermarkets. To make your own, combine 2 tbsp (20 g) garlic powder, 1 tbsp (18 g) salt, 1 tbsp (10 g) onion powder, 1 tsp (1 g) dried oregano leaves, 1 tsp (2 g) freshly ground black pepper, 1 tsp (2 g) ground cumin, ½ tsp (1 g) ground turmeric in a bowl, whisking well. Measure 1 tbsp (18 g) for this recipe and store remaining in an airtight container or jar for up to 6 months.

¼ cup	avocado oil or olive oil	57 g
3	stalks celery, diced	3
2	carrots, diced	2
2	cloves garlic, minced	2
1	large onion, diced	1
½ tsp	garlic salt	3 g
5 cups	chicken stock or broth	1.18 L
1 tbsp	adobo seasoning (see Tip, left)	18 g
½ tsp	ground cumin	1 g
2	boneless skinless chicken breasts, cut into bite-size pieces	2
1	can (28 oz / 796 g) fire-roasted diced tomatoes, with juice	1
1	can (4 oz / 113 g) chopped green chilies	1
1	can (14 to 15 oz / 398 to 425 g) black beans, drained and rinsed	1
1 cup	coarsely crumbled tortilla chips	50 g
1 cup	milk	240 g
1 cup	shredded Tex-Mex blend cheese or jalapeño Jack cheese	112 g

TOPPINGS, OPTIONAL

Shredded Tex-Mex blend cheese or jalapeño Jack cheese

Tortilla chips

Avocados, sliced

Fresh cilantro leaves

Limes, cut into wedges

Stovetop Method

1. In a large pot, heat oil over medium-high heat. Add celery, carrots, garlic, onion and garlic salt. Cook, stirring, for about 5 minutes or until tender. Add stock, adobo seasoning, cumin, chicken, tomatoes, green chilies, black beans and crumbled tortilla chips. Bring to a low boil. Reduce heat and simmer, stirring occasionally, for about 20 minutes or until chicken is no longer pink inside and soup is thickened. Remove from heat.

2. Stir in milk and cheese until blended and cheese is melted.

3. Ladle soup into bowls. Top with cheese, tortilla chips, avocado and cilantro, as desired. Serve with lime wedges.

Pressure Cooker Method

1. In a pressure cooker, heat oil over medium-high heat. Add celery, carrots, garlic, onion and garlic salt. Cook, stirring, for about 5 minutes or until tender. Add stock, adobo seasoning, cumin, chicken, tomatoes, green chilies, black beans and crumbled tortilla chips. Lock the pressure lid into place. Heat the pot over high heat and bring pressure to High. Cook for 5 minutes, adjusting heat as necessary to maintain pressure. Remove from heat and let pressure release naturally. The chicken should be no longer pink inside. If not, return to pressure and cook in 2-minute increments until done.

2. Uncover pot. Stir in milk and cheese until blended and cheese is melted.

3. Ladle soup into bowls. Top with cheese, tortilla chips, avocado and cilantro, as desired. Serve with lime wedges.

Bread Pairing

Cheddar Chili Bread Sticks (page 40)

Creamy Adobo Chicken Soup (page 128) and Cheddar Chili Bread Sticks (page 40)

Green Chili Chicken Soup

This soup is a family favorite, especially when served in homemade bread bowls (see page 35). I use canned chopped mild green chilies. They are slightly spicy but not hot. If you want to turn up the heat a bit, there are hot varieties of canned green chilies that can be used.

MAKES 6 TO 8 SERVINGS

- Large pot or minimum 6-qt (6 L) pressure cooker

Tips

The metric weights have been calculated as precise conversions from imperial volumes. For ease, you can round the quantities up or down slightly in this soup and still get good results.

This soup can be made ahead and refrigerated for up to 3 days, adding milk and cheese just before serving. See page 31 for detailed instructions.

2	large bone-in chicken breasts (or 3 lb / 1.36 kg whole chicken)	2
8 cups	cold water	1.89 L
2 tsp	sweet paprika	4 g
$\frac{1}{2}$ tsp	salt	3 g
$\frac{1}{2}$ tsp	freshly ground black pepper	1 g
$\frac{1}{2}$ tsp	garlic salt	3 g
$\frac{1}{4}$ tsp	ground cumin	0.5 g
2	bay leaves	2
4 cups	cubed red potatoes	520 g
$1\frac{1}{2}$ cups	chopped onions	195 g
$\frac{1}{2}$ cup	thinly sliced carrot	64 g
3	cans (each 4 oz / 113 g) chopped green chilies	1
1	can (14 to 15 oz / 398 to 425 g) diced tomatoes	1
1	can (10 oz / 284 g) diced tomatoes with green chilies (with juice)	1
2 tsp	minced fresh cilantro	2 g
$\frac{1}{2}$ cup	milk	120 g
6 tbsp	shredded sharp (old) Cheddar cheese	42 g

Stovetop Method

1. In a large pot, combine chicken, water, paprika, salt, pepper, garlic salt, cumin, bay leaves, potatoes, onions and carrots. Bring to a boil over high heat. Reduce heat and simmer, stirring occasionally, for 20 to 30 minutes for breasts (or for about 1½ hours for whole chicken) or until an instant-read thermometer inserted into thickest part of chicken registers 165°F (74°C) and potatoes are tender. Remove from heat.

2. Using tongs, transfer chicken to a bowl and remove bay leaves; discard bay leaves. Let chicken cool slightly, then remove skin, if necessary, and meat from bones; discard skin and bones. Shred into bite-size pieces.

3. Add shredded chicken back to soup. Stir in green chilies, diced tomatoes, tomatoes with green chilies and cilantro. Bring to a simmer over medium heat, stirring occasionally. Remove from heat; stir in milk.

4. Ladle soup into bowls. Top with cheese and serve.

Pressure Cooker Method

1. In a pressure cooker, combine chicken, water, paprika, salt, pepper, garlic salt, cumin, bay leaves, potatoes, onions and carrots. Lock the pressure lid into place. Heat the pot over high heat and bring pressure to High. Cook for 10 minutes for chicken breasts (or 15 minutes for a whole chicken), adjusting heat as necessary to maintain pressure. Remove from heat and let pressure release naturally. The potatoes should be tender. Test the chicken to ensure an instant-read thermometer inserted into thickest part of chicken registers 165°F (74°C). If not, return to pressure and cook in 2-minute increments (or 5 minutes for whole chicken) until done.

2. Uncover pot. Using tongs, transfer chicken to a bowl and remove bay leaves; discard bay leaves. Let chicken cool slightly, then remove meat skin, if necessary, from bones; discard and skin bones. Shred into bite-size pieces.

3. Add shredded chicken back to soup. Stir in green chilies, diced tomatoes, tomatoes with green chilies and cilantro. Bring to a simmer over medium heat, stirring occasionally. Remove from heat; stir in milk.

4. Ladle soup into bowls. Top with cheese and serve.

Bread Pairing

Bread Bowls (page 35)

Green Chili Chicken Soup (page 132)
in Bread Bowls (page 35)

French Onion Chicken Soup

This versatile version of French onion soup begins with the usual slow sautéing of onions but surprises with the rewarding addition of chicken. Serve topped with cheese but with crusty bread alongside instead of in the bowl. We also enjoy it served over brown rice.

MAKES 4 SERVINGS

- Large, deep skillet or saucepan or minimum $4\frac{1}{4}$-qt (4.5 L) pressure cooker (preferably skillet style, see Tip, below)

3 tbsp	extra virgin olive oil, divided	42 g
1	large onion, thinly sliced	1
2 tsp	chopped fresh thyme leaves (or 1 tsp / 1 g dried thyme)	2 g
	Salt and freshly ground black pepper	
2	cloves garlic, finely chopped	2
$1\frac{1}{2}$ lbs	boneless skinless chicken breasts, cut into 1-inch (2.5 cm) pieces	681 g
2 tbsp	freshly milled hard or soft white wheat flour	18 g
$\frac{1}{2}$ tsp	dried oregano leaves	0.5 g
$1\frac{1}{2}$ cups	beef stock or broth (see Tip, left)	354 g
1 cup	shredded Gruyère cheese	113 g
	Chopped fresh parsley (optional)	

Tips

A wide, skillet-style pressure cooker is ideal for caramelizing the onions for this soup. If you don't have one, you can use a large skillet for step 1, then transfer the onion mixture to the pressure cooker for step 3. Be sure to use a little of the stock to deglaze the skillet and scrape up all of the browned bits (and flavor) to pour into the soup. If using a narrower pressure cooker for step 1, the onions may need a little longer to cook.

Classic French onion soup is made with beef stock for its rich flavor, so I've used that here along with the chicken. You can substitute the beef with chicken stock in this recipe if you prefer, but keep in mind the overall taste of the soup will be much milder.

Stovetop Method

1. In a large, deep skillet, heat 2 tbsp (28 g) oil over medium heat. Stir in onion and thyme; season with salt and pepper to taste. Reduce heat to medium-low and cook, stirring occasionally, for 20 to 25 minutes or until onions are very soft and caramelized. Add garlic and cook, stirring, for about 1 minute, until fragrant. Transfer to a small bowl; set aside. Wipe skillet clean.

2. In a large bowl, season chicken with salt and pepper to taste. Add flour and oregano; toss to coat.

3. Return skillet to medium-high heat. Add remaining 1 tbsp (14 g) oil and swirl to coat. Add chicken and cook, stirring gently, to brown on all sides and to cook slightly. Stir in stock. Return onion mixture to skillet. Bring to a simmer, stirring to scrape any brown bits from the bottom of the pot.

4. Cover skillet, reduce heat to low and simmer, stirring occasionally, for about 10 minutes or until chicken is no longer pink inside.

5. Uncover skillet. Sprinkle with shredded cheese. Cover and let stand until cheese is melted.

6. Ladle into bowls and serve garnished with parsley, if desired.

Pressure Cooker Method

1. In a pressure cooker, heat 2 tbsp (28 g) oil over medium heat. Stir in onion and thyme; season with salt and pepper to taste. Reduce heat to medium-low and cook, stirring occasionally, for 20 to 25 minutes or until onions are very soft and caramelized. Add garlic and cook, stirring, for about 1 minute, until fragrant. Transfer to a small bowl; set aside. Wipe pot clean.

2. In a large bowl, season chicken with salt and pepper to taste. Add flour and oregano; toss to coat.

3. Return pot to medium-high heat. Add remaining 1 tbsp (14 g) oil and swirl to coat. Add chicken and cook, stirring gently, to brown on all sides and to cook slightly. Stir in stock. Return onion mixture to skillet. Bring to a simmer, stirring to scrape any brown bits from the bottom of the pot.

4. Lock the pressure lid into place. Heat the pot over high heat and bring pressure to High. Cook for 5 minutes, adjusting heat as necessary to maintain pressure. Remove from heat and let pressure release naturally or quick-release the pressure. The chicken should be no longer pink inside. If not, return to pressure and cook in 2-minute increments until done.

5. Uncover pot. Sprinkle with shredded cheese. Cover and let stand until cheese is melted.

6. Ladle into bowls and serve garnished with parsley, if desired.

Bread Pairing

Crusty No-Knead Bread (page 48)

French Onion Chicken Soup (page 136) and Crusty No-Knead Bread (page 48)

Chicken Corn Chowder (page 140) and
Cheddar-Jalapeño Bread (page 37)

Creamy Italian Sausage Pasta Soup

This rich and creamy soup is packed with traditional Italian-inspired ingredients that add up to a satisfyingly delicious meal. It's a favorite in the soup and bread classes I teach, as it's so quick and easy. I'm sure will soon be a favorite for your family as well.

MAKES 6 SERVINGS

- Large pot or minimum 6-qt (6 L) pressure cooker

Tips

Use your favorite diced tomatoes in this recipe, plain or seasoned. I love the variety with fire-roasted garlic.

I like to use equal amounts of mild and hot Italian chicken sausage. This gives just a slight heat to the soup.

When pressure cooking, if you prefer to let the pressure release naturally, in step 2, reduce the cooking time to 2 minutes.

1 to 2 tbsp	extra virgin olive oil	14 to 28 g
1 lb	Italian chicken or turkey sausage (casings removed or bulk)	454 g
1	small onion, diced	1
2	cloves garlic, minced	2
1 tsp	dried Italian seasoning (or combination of dried oregano, basil and thyme)	1 g
	Salt and freshly ground black pepper	
1	can (14 to 15 oz / 398 to 425 g) diced tomatoes (see Tip, left), lightly drained	1
4 cups	chicken stock or broth	944 mL
1 cup	small pasta, such as elbow macaroni or fusilli	125 g
1 cup	heavy or whipping (35%) cream	240 g
1 cup	shredded Parmesan cheese	100 g
	Chopped fresh parsley (optional)	

Stovetop Method

1. In a large pot, heat enough oil over medium-high heat to make a thin coating; brown sausage meat, breaking up with a spoon into small clumps and stirring, for about 10 to 12 minutes or until thoroughly browned. Add onion, garlic, Italian seasoning, $\frac{1}{2}$ tsp (3 g) salt and $\frac{1}{2}$ tsp (1 g) pepper; cook, stirring, for 3 minutes, until onion is softened.

2. Stir in tomatoes and stock; increase heat to high and bring to a boil. Stir in pasta; reduce heat and boil gently, stirring occasionally, for 5 to 7 minutes, until pasta is al dente.

3. Stir in cream and Parmesan; heat over medium heat, stirring, just until steaming. Season with salt and pepper to taste.

4. Ladle soup into bowls and garnish with parsley, if desired.

Pressure Cooker Method

1. In a pressure cooker, heat enough oil over medium-high heat to make a thin coating; brown sausage meat, breaking up with a spoon into small clumps and stirring, for about 10 to 12 minutes or until thoroughly browned. Add onion, garlic, Italian seasoning, $\frac{1}{2}$ tsp (3 g) salt and $\frac{1}{2}$ tsp (1 g) pepper; cook, stirring, for 3 minutes, until onion is softened.

2. Stir in tomatoes and stock; increase heat to high and bring to a boil. Stir in pasta. Lock the pressure lid into place. Heat the pot over high heat and bring pressure to High. Cook for 3 minutes, adjusting heat as necessary to maintain pressure. Remove from heat and quick-release the pressure (see Tip, opposite left). The pasta should be cooked al dente. If not, return to pressure and cook or 1 minute longer or until done.

3. Uncover pot. Stir in cream and Parmesan; heat over medium heat, stirring, just until steaming. Season with salt and pepper to taste.

4. Ladle soup into bowls and garnish with parsley, if desired.

Bread Pairing

Ciabatta Bread (page 62)

Creamy Italian Sausage Pasta Soup (page 144) and Ciabatta Bread (page 62)

Spicy Lentil and Barley Soup
with Chicken and Italian Sausage

Don't be surprised that there is no salt in the ingredients list. The flavors are perfect without it. But you can always add it at the end if you want a little more saltiness.

MAKES 6 TO 8 SERVINGS

- Large pot or minimum 6-qt (6 L) pressure cooker

Tips

If you cannot find chili-flavored salsa, add 1 tbsp (18 g) chili powder along with a jar of your favorite prepared salsa.

The metric weights have been calculated as precise conversions from imperial volumes. For ease, you can round the quantities up or down slightly in this soup and still get good results.

½ lb	Italian turkey or chicken sausage (casings removed or bulk)	227 g
1 to 2 tbsp	olive oil	14 to 28 g
1	onion, chopped	1
3	cloves garlic, minced	3
⅓ cup	hulled barley	60 g
2	boneless chicken breasts (about 1 lb / 454 g)	2
1 cup	dried green lentils	220 g
½ cup	fresh cilantro leaves	24 g
8 cups	chicken stock or broth	1.89 L
1½ cups	drained cooked black beans, see page 29 (or one 14 to 15 oz / 398 to 425 g can black beans, drained and rinsed)	270 g
1	jar (about 12 oz / 340 g) chili-flavored salsa (see Tip, left)	1
1 lb	fresh spinach, stems removed	454 g

Stovetop Method

1. In large pot, heat 1 tbsp (14 g) of the oil over medium-high heat; brown sausage meat, breaking up with a spoon until crumbled and stirring, for about 10 to 12 minutes or until thoroughly browned. Using a slotted spoon, transfer meat to a bowl; set aside.

2. Add more oil to pot, as necessary. Add onion, garlic and barley; cook over medium heat, stirring, for about 5 minutes or until onion is soft and barley is toasted.

3. Add chicken breasts, lentils, cilantro and stock; bring to a simmer. Cover, reduce heat to low and simmer, stirring occasionally, for about 1 hour or until barley is tender and an instant-read thermometer inserted into thickest part of chicken registers 165°F (74°C).

4. Uncover pot. Using tongs, transfer chicken breasts to a plate and let cool slightly. Shred into bite-size pieces.

5. Return pot to medium heat. Return chicken and sausage to pot; stir in black beans and salsa. Simmer until heated through. Stir in spinach, just until wilted.

6. Ladle soup into bowls.

Pressure Cooker Method

1. In a pressure cooker, heat 1 tbsp (14 g) of the oil over medium-high heat; brown sausage meat, breaking up with a spoon until crumbled and stirring, for about 10 to 12 minutes or until thoroughly browned. Using a slotted spoon, transfer meat to a bowl; set aside.

2. Add more oil to pot, as necessary. Add onion, garlic and barley; cook over medium heat, stirring, for about 5 minutes or until onion is soft and barley is toasted.

3. Add chicken breasts, lentils, cilantro and stock. Lock the pressure lid into place. Heat the pot over high heat and bring pressure to High. Cook for 20 minutes, adjusting heat as necessary to maintain pressure. Remove from heat and quick-release the pressure. Test the chicken to ensure an instant-read thermometer inserted into thickest part of chicken registers 165°F (74°C). If not, return to pressure and cook in 2-minute increments until done.

4. Uncover pot. Using tongs, transfer chicken breasts to a plate and let cool slightly. Shred into bite-size pieces.

5. Return pot to medium heat. Return chicken and sausage to pot; stir in black beans and salsa. Simmer until heated through. Stir in spinach, just until wilted.

6. Ladle soup into bowls.

Bread Pairing

Cheddar Chili Bread Sticks (page 40)

Spicy Lentil and Barley Soup with Chicken and Italian Sausage (page 148)
and Cheddar Chili Bread Sticks (page 40)

Potato Soup with Italian Sausage (page 152)
and Parmesan Pull-Apart Rolls (page 43)

Turkey Spinach Gnocchi Soup

My daughter Abby called while I was working on this book. She shared this recipe with me, saying that whenever she makes it, it's a favorite with all who taste it, especially her youngest sibling's husband, James. Gnocchi, soft Italian dumplings made traditionally with mashed potatoes, provide a nice change from pasta in this soup.

MAKES 6 SERVINGS

- Large pot or Dutch oven

Tips

Plum tomatoes, also called Roma tomatoes, are a meaty, paste variety of tomato. They have fewer seeds and less juice so are the best choice for this soup. If not available, other varieties will work; scoop out the seeds and juice before dicing to avoid adding too much liquid to the soup.

You can find packaged gnocchi in various sections in the grocery store: in the refrigerator or deli section, on the shelves with dried pasta or in the freezer section. Adjust the cooking time in step 3 according to the package directions, as necessary, adding spinach for the last 5 minutes if cooking time is longer.

⅓ cup	unsalted butter	76 g
1 lb	ground turkey	454 g
1	large onion, chopped	1
¼ cup	freshly milled soft wheat flour (preferably white wheat)	31 g
6 cups	chicken stock or broth	1.42 L
2	large fresh plum (Roma) tomatoes (or 3 medium), diced	2
2	sprigs fresh rosemary	2
	Grated zest of 1 lemon	
2 tbsp	dried Italian seasoning	6 g
1 tbsp	salt	18 g
1 cup	heavy or whipping (35%) cream	240 g
1	package (16 oz / 454 g) gnocchi (see Tip, left)	1
1 cup	lightly packed fresh spinach, chopped	30 g

Stovetop Method

1. In large pot or Dutch oven, melt butter over medium-high heat. Add turkey and onion; cook, stirring and breaking up meat with a spoon, for about 5 minutes, until meat is cooked through and onions are softened.

2. Sprinkle in flour; cook, stirring, for about 2 minutes until evenly combined. Gradually pour in stock while whisking. Cook, stirring, for 1 to 2 minutes or until thickened. Stir in tomatoes, rosemary, lemon zest, Italian seasoning and salt. Cover, reduce heat to low and simmer, stirring occasionally, for about 10 minutes, until tomatoes are softened.

3. Uncover pot. Stir in heavy cream, gnocchi and spinach. Simmer, stirring once, for about 5 minutes (for fresh gnocchi, see Tip, opposite left) or until gnocchi floats to the surface and is tender.

4. Ladle soup into bowls.

Bread Pairing

Sun-Dried Tomato, Basil and Garlic Filled Bread (page 38)

Turkey Spinach Gnocchi Soup (page 156) and
Sun-Dried Tomato, Basil and Garlic Filled Bread (page 38)

Cheeseburger Soup

This satisfying soup has all the flavors of a delicious cheeseburger stirred into one pot. It's a family and potluck dinner favorite.

MAKES 6 SERVINGS

- Large pot or minimum 6-qt (6 L) pressure cooker
- Medium saucepan

Tip

The metric weights have been calculated as precise conversions from imperial volumes. For ease, you can round the quantities up or down slightly in this soup and still get good results.

4 tbsp	unsalted butter, divided	56 g
1 lb	lean ground beef	454 g
1	small onion, diced	1
2	stalks celery, diced	2 g
½ cup	diced carrot	64 g
1	clove garlic, minced	1
2 cups	diced potatoes	260 g
1 tsp	dried Italian seasoning or dried basil leaves	1 g
	Salt	
4 cups	chicken stock or broth	944 mL
¼ cup	freshly milled soft white wheat flour	31 g
1½ cups	whole milk	360 g
2 cups	shredded Cheddar cheese	224 g
¼ cup	ketchup	60 g
2 tbsp	prepared yellow mustard	30 g
	Freshly ground black pepper	
	Chopped dill pickles	

Stovetop Method

1. In a large pot, melt 1 tbsp (14 g) of the butter over medium heat. Add ground beef and cook, stirring and breaking up into chunks, until browned. Add onions, celery, carrot and garlic; cook, stirring, for about 5 minutes, until vegetables are tender.

2. Stir in potatoes, Italian seasoning, 1 tsp (6 g) salt and stock. Increase heat to high and bring to a boil. Cover, reduce heat to low and simmer, stirring occasionally, for about 20 minutes, until potatoes are tender.

3. Meanwhile, in a saucepan, melt remaining 3 tbsp (42 g) butter over medium heat. Whisk in flour; cook, whisking, for 1 to 2 minutes. (Do not let brown.) Gradually pour in milk while whisking. Remove from heat.

4. Uncover soup. Gradually whisk in milk mixture. Cook over medium heat, stirring often, for 3 to 4 minutes until soup is thickened. Reduce heat to low. Stir in cheese, ketchup and mustard; heat, stirring, until cheese melts. Season with salt and pepper to taste.

5. Ladle soup into bowls and garnish with dill pickles, if desired.

Pressure Cooker Method

1. In a pressure cooker, melt 1 tbsp (14 g) of the butter over medium heat. Add ground beef and cook, stirring and breaking up into chunks, until browned. Add onions, celery, carrot and garlic; cook, stirring, for about 5 minutes, until vegetables are tender.

2. Stir in potatoes, Italian seasoning, 1 tsp (6 g) salt and stock; bring to a boil. Stir once. Lock the pressure lid into place. Heat the pot over high heat and bring pressure to High. Cook for 5 minutes, adjusting heat to maintain pressure as necessary. Remove from heat and let pressure release naturally or quick-release the pressure.

3. Meanwhile, in a saucepan, melt remaining 3 tbsp (42 g) butter over medium heat. Whisk in flour; cook, whisking, for 1 to 2 minutes. (Do not let brown.) Gradually pour in milk while whisking. Remove from heat.

4. Uncover soup. Gradually whisk in milk mixture. Cook over medium heat, stirring often, for 3 to 4 minutes until soup is thickened. Reduce heat to low. Stir in cheese, ketchup and mustard; heat, stirring, until cheese melts. Season with salt and pepper to taste.

5. Ladle soup into bowls and garnish with dill pickles, if desired.

Bread Pairing

Dill and Feta Cheese Drop Biscuits (page 79)

Cheeseburger Soup (page 160) and
Dill and Feta Cheese Drop Biscuits (page 79)

Beef and Mushroom Barley Soup

This rich and flavorful soup comes together easily and quickly, especially in a pressure cooker. It is a hearty soup that will satisfy big appetites. Double your taste for umami by pairing with a savory slice of Mushroom Cheese Bread.

MAKES 4 SERVINGS

- Large pot or minimum 6-qt (6 L) pressure cooker

Tip

There are several brands of dried mushroom seasoning powder available to choose from. Look for one that has dried mushroom powder, garlic and salt as the key ingredients. Or you can substitute 1 clove of minced garlic and another herb seasoning blend or umami seasoning, if you prefer.

2 tbsp	olive oil	28 g
1	onion, thinly sliced	1
8 oz	portobello mushrooms, stems trimmed, sliced	227 g
8 oz	beef stew meat, cut into $\frac{3}{4}$-inch (2 cm) pieces	227 g
$\frac{1}{2}$ cup	hulled barley	90 g
1 tbsp	dried mushroom seasoning powder (see Tip, left)	8 g
$\frac{1}{2}$ tsp	salt	3 g
4 cups	beef or mushroom stock or broth	944 mL
	Freshly ground black pepper	

Stovetop Method

1. In a large pot, heat oil over medium heat. Cook onions, stirring, for about 5 minutes, until tender but not browned. Stir in sliced mushrooms, meat, barley, mushroom seasoning powder and salt. Cook, stirring, for 2 to 3 minutes. Add stock and bring to a boil over high heat.

2. Cover, reduce heat to low and simmer, stirring occasionally, for 1 hour or until beef and barley are tender. Remove from heat. Let stand for about 10 minutes to allow barley to absorb more liquid.

3. Season soup with pepper to taste and ladle into bowls.

Pressure Cooker Method

1. In a pressure cooker, heat oil over medium heat. Cook onions, stirring, for about 5 minutes, until tender but not browned. Stir in sliced mushrooms, meat, barley, mushroom seasoning powder and salt. Cook, stirring, for 2 to 3 minutes. Add stock.

2. Lock the pressure lid into place. Heat the pot over high heat and bring pressure to High. Cook for 18 minutes, adjusting heat to maintain pressure as necessary. Remove from heat and let pressure release naturally. The beef and barley should be tender. If not, return to pressure and cook in 2-minute increments until done.

3. Uncover pot. Season soup with pepper to taste and ladle into bowls.

Bread Pairing

Mushroom Cheese Bread (page 44)

Beef and Mushroom Barley Soup (page 164)
and Mushroom Cheese Bread (page 44)

Beef and Barley Soup
with Roasted Vegetables

This hearty soup contains all the flavors of fall. The little extra effort of roasting the vegetables adds a depth of flavor to what is quite a simple soup.

MAKES 6 TO 8 SERVINGS

- Rimmed baking sheet
- Large pot or minimum 6-qt (6 L) pressure cooker

Tip

You can use $\frac{1}{4}$ cup (31 g) freshly milled soft wheat flour or $\frac{1}{4}$ cup (33 g) freshly milled spelt flour in place of the barley flour.

Preheat oven to 425°F (220°C)

ROASTED VEGETABLES

2 cups	cubed peeled butternut squash	280 g
2	large carrots, cut in $\frac{1}{2}$-inch (1 cm) slices	2
1	large russet potato, cubed	1
	Olive oil	
	Salt and freshly ground black pepper	

SOUP

$\frac{1}{4}$ cup	freshly milled barley flour (see Tip, left)	25 g
1 tsp	salt	6 g
$\frac{1}{2}$ tsp	freshly ground black pepper	1 g
1 lb	beef stew meat, cut into $\frac{3}{4}$-inch (2 cm) cubes	454 g
3 tbsp	olive oil, divided	42 g
1	large portobello mushroom, stem removed, cap chopped	1
1	bulb fennel, chopped	1
1	onion, chopped	1
2	cloves garlic, minced	2
8 cups	beef stock or broth	1.89 L
$\frac{2}{3}$ cup	hulled barley	120 g
2 cups	water	472 g
2 tsp	fresh thyme leaves	2 g
Pinch	ground nutmeg	Pinch
$\frac{1}{4}$ cup	minced fresh parsley (optional)	12 g

Stovetop Method

1. **Roasted Vegetables:** On a rimmed baking sheet, combine squash, carrots and potato. Drizzle with olive oil and sprinkle with salt and pepper to taste. Toss to coat evenly and spread out in a single layer. Roast in preheated oven for about 20 minutes or until browned and slightly tender.

2. **Soup:** Meanwhile, in a small bowl, combine flour, salt and pepper. In a medium bowl, sprinkle flour mixture over beef and toss to coat.

3. In a large pot, heat 2 tbsp (28 g) of the oil over medium heat. Add beef and cook, stirring, until brown on all sides. Transfer to a bowl and set aside.

4. Return pot to medium heat and add 1 tbsp (14 g) oil. Add mushroom, fennel and onion; cook, stirring, for 4 to 5 minutes or until tender. Add garlic; cook, stirring, for 1 minute. Add stock and bring to a simmer, scraping up brown bits from bottom of the pot. Stir in barley, water and reserved beef with accumulated juices.

5. Bring soup to a boil over high heat. Cover, reduce heat to low and simmer, stirring occasionally, for 1 hour until beef and barley are tender.

6. Uncover pot. Stir in thyme, nutmeg and roasted vegetables. Simmer over medium heat, stirring once, for about 5 minutes to blend the flavors.

7. Ladle soup into bowls and sprinkle with parsley, if desired.

Pressure Cooker Method

1. **Roasted Vegetables:** On a rimmed baking sheet, combine squash, carrots and potato. Drizzle with olive oil and sprinkle with salt and pepper to taste. Toss to coat evenly and spread out in a single layer. Roast in preheated oven for about 20 minutes or until browned and slightly tender.

2. **Soup:** Meanwhile, in a small bowl, combine flour, salt and pepper. In a medium bowl, sprinkle flour mixture over beef and toss to coat.

3. In a pressure cooker, heat 2 tbsp (28 g) of the oil over medium heat. Add beef and cook, stirring, until brown on all sides. Transfer to a bowl and set aside.

4. Return pot to medium heat and add 1 tbsp (14 g) oil. Add mushroom, fennel and onion; cook, stirring, for 4 to 5 minutes or until tender. Add garlic; cook, stirring, for 1 minute. Add stock and bring to a simmer, scraping up brown bits from bottom of the pot. Stir in barley, water and reserved beef with accumulated juices.

5. Lock the pressure lid into place. Heat the pot over high heat and bring pressure to High. Cook for 18 minutes, adjusting heat to maintain pressure as necessary. Remove from heat and let pressure release naturally. The beef and barley should be tender. If not, return to pressure and cook in 2-minute increments until done.

6. Uncover pot. Stir in thyme, nutmeg and roasted vegetables. Simmer over medium heat, stirring once, for about 5 minutes to blend the flavors.

7. Ladle soup into bowls and sprinkle with parsley, if desired.

Bread Pairing

Easy Drop Biscuits (page 76)

Beef and Barley Soup with Roasted Vegetables (page 168) and Easy Drop Biscuits (page 76)

Beef and Barley Soup
with Red Wine and Pesto

Tomatoes, pesto and baby kale give this otherwise classic beef soup a vegetable boost and a flavorful twist. It's hearty, delicious and very filling, using two of my favorite soup ingredient combinations — beef and barley.

MAKES 4 TO 6 SERVINGS

- Large pot or minimum 6-qt (6 L) pressure cooker

Tip

When using canned tomatoes, I like to choose those with seasonings appropriate to the flavors of my recipe such as in this one with basil, garlic and oregano. You can certainly use a can of plain diced tomatoes and add your own extra seasonings as desired.

1 lb	boneless beef chuck (blade) roast, cut into $\frac{3}{4}$-inch (2 cm) cubes	454 g
	Salt and freshly ground black pepper	
2 tbsp	olive oil, divided	28 g
$1\frac{1}{2}$ cups	thickly sliced carrots	128 g
1 cup	chopped onions	130 g
$\frac{1}{2}$ cup	dry red wine	118 g
$\frac{1}{2}$ cup	hulled barley	90 g
4 cups	beef stock or broth	944 mL
1	can (14 to 15 oz / 398 to 425 g) seasoned diced tomatoes (with basil, garlic and oregano)	
$\frac{1}{4}$ cup	basil pesto	60 g
5 oz	baby kale leaves	142 g
	Additional basil pesto (optional)	

Stovetop Method

1. Pat beef dry and sprinkle with ½ tsp (3 g) salt and ½ tsp (1 g) pepper. In a large pot, heat 1 tbsp (14 g) of the oil over medium-high heat. Add beef and cook, stirring, for about 4 minutes, until brown on all sides. Transfer to a bowl and set aside.

2. Add remaining oil to the pot. Add carrots and onions; cook for 3 to 4 minutes, stirring occasionally, until tender. Pour in wine and bring to a simmer, scraping up brown bits from bottom of the pot. Stir in barley, stock, tomatoes and pesto.

3. Bring to a simmer over high heat. Cover, reduce heat to low and simmer, stirring occasionally, for 1 hour until beef and barley are tender.

4. Uncover pot. Stir in kale until wilted. Season with salt and pepper to taste.

5. Ladle soup into bowls and drizzle with pesto, as desired.

Pressure Cooker Method

1. Pat beef dry and sprinkle with ½ tsp (3 g) salt and ½ tsp (1 g) pepper. In a pressure cooker, heat 1 tbsp (14 g) of the oil over medium-high heat. Add beef and cook, stirring, for about 4 minutes, until brown on all sides. Transfer to a bowl and set aside.

2. Add remaining oil to the pot. Add carrots and onions; cook for 3 to 4 minutes, stirring occasionally, until tender. Pour in wine and bring to a simmer, scraping up brown bits from bottom of the pot. Stir in barley, stock, tomatoes and pesto.

3. Lock the pressure lid into place. Heat the pot over high heat and bring pressure to High. Cook for 18 minutes, adjusting heat to maintain pressure as necessary. Remove from heat and let pressure release naturally. The beef and barley should be tender. If not, return to pressure and cook in 2-minute increments until done.

4. Uncover pot. Stir in kale until wilted. Season with salt and pepper to taste.

5. Ladle soup into bowls and drizzle with pesto, as desired.

Bread Pairing

Crusty No-Knead Spelt Bread (page 51)

Beef and Barley Soup with Red Wine and Pesto (page 172)
and Crusty No-Knead Spelt Bread (page 51)

Easy Beef Stroganoff Soup

Why not make it soup? This is a delicious, aromatic variation of the perfect comfort food. And it is ready in about 15 minutes when cooked in a pressure cooker.

MAKES 4 TO 6 SERVINGS

- Medium pot or minimum 4½-qt (4.5 L) pressure cooker

Tip

For the pressure cooker, in step 2, if you want to let the pressure naturally release, reduce the cook time to 3 minutes.

1 to 2 tbsp	oil	14 to 28 g
1½ lbs	ground beef	681 g
8 oz	mushrooms, sliced	227 g
2 tbsp	seasoning salt	34 g
4 cups	beef stock or broth	944 mL
2 cups	whole-grain elbow macaroni or other small pasta	250 g
1 to 1½ cups	sour cream	245 to 368 g

Stovetop Method

1. In a medium pot, heat enough oil to make a thin layer over the bottom of the pot over high heat. Add ground beef and mushrooms; cook, stirring and breaking up meat into chunks, until browned. Sprinkle with seasoning salt. Add the stock and bring to a boil. Stir in pasta.

2. Cover, reduce heat to low and simmer, stirring occasionally, for 10 for 12 minutes until pasta is tender.

3. Remove from heat. Stir in sour cream to taste. Ladle into bowls.

Pressure Cooker Method

1. In a pressure cooker, heat enough oil to make a thin layer over the bottom of the pot over high heat. Add ground beef and mushrooms; cook, stirring and breaking up meat into chunks, until browned. Sprinkle with seasoning salt. Add the stock and bring to a boil. Stir in pasta.

2. Lock the pressure lid into place. Heat the pot over high heat and bring the pressure to High. Cook for 5 minutes (see Tip, opposite left), adjusting heat to maintain pressure as necessary. Remove from heat and quick-release the pressure. The pasta should be tender. If not, return to pressure and cook for 1 to 2 minutes longer until done.

3. Uncover pot. Stir in sour cream to taste. Ladle into bowls.

Bread Pairing

Roasted Carrot Sage Biscuits (page 84)

Easy Beef Stroganoff Soup (page 176) and Roasted Carrot Sage Biscuits (page 84)

Patty Melt Soup (page 180) and
Grilled Swiss on Rye Sandwiches

Grilled Swiss on Rye Sandwiches

Who doesn't love a good grilled cheese sandwich? I like to change up a traditional grilled cheese by using rye bread and Swiss cheese for a stand-alone sandwich. But a classic Patty Melt is by far one of my favorite hamburgers. So adding these petite grilled cheese sandwiches to this soup gives me all the flavors of my favorite burger.

MAKES 6 SANDWICHES

- Large skillet

2 tbsp	butter, softened or melted	28 g
$\frac{1}{2}$ tsp	dry mustard	1 g
$\frac{1}{4}$ tsp	onion salt	1 g
12	slices Rye Baguettes (recipe, page 55)	12
6	Swiss cheese slices, broken into quarters	6

1. In a small bowl, combine butter, mustard and onion salt. Arrange bread slices in a single layer on a work surface; spread one side of each slice with butter mixture. Flip half of the bread slices over and stack 4 cheese slice quarters on top of each. Place remaining bread slices on top with the buttered side out.

2. Heat a large skillet over medium heat. Add sandwiches, in batches as necessary, and cook for about 2 to 3 minutes per side or until browned and cheese is melted, adjusting heat as necessary to avoid burning.

Creamy Mexican Potato Soup
with Adobo Steak and Salsa

This is not your usual steak and potatoes meal. In this new classic, the main ingredients are combined with a Mexican-inspired twist. Start with a cheesy potato soup, then layer on the flavors with Adobo Rubbed Steak, fresh pico-style salsa, and a squeeze of lime to make each steaming bowl a full-meal deal.

MAKES 8 SERVINGS

- Large pot or minimum 6-qt (6 L) pressure cooker
- Small saucepan
- Potato masher

Tip

This soup can be made ahead through step 3, stirring cream mixture into soup (adding cheese until just before serving) and refrigerated for up to 3 days. See page 31 for detailed instructions to cool, store and reheat. Make the steak and salsa the day of serving.

2 tbsp	extra virgin olive oil	28 g
1 cup	chopped onion (about 1 medium onion)	130 g
½ cup	chopped celery	60 g
8	cloves garlic, minced	8
1 tbsp	ground cumin	6 g
2 tsp	dried oregano leaves, preferably Mexican oregano	2 g
1 tsp	ground coriander	2 g
¼ tsp	cayenne pepper	0.5 g
2 lbs	red potatoes, cubed	908 g
1 tsp	salt	6 g
4 cups	chicken stock or broth	944 mL
2 tbsp	unsalted butter	28 g
2 tbsp	freshly milled soft white wheat flour	16 g
1½ cups	half-and-half (10%) cream	360 g

TO SERVE

12 oz	hot pepper Jack cheese, shredded	340 g
½ cup	sour cream	123 g
2 tsp	ground cumin or taco seasoning	4 g
	Salt and freshly ground black pepper	
	Adobo Rubbed Steak (recipe, page 186)	
	Brad's Incredible Salsa (recipe, page 187)	
	Lime wedges	

Stovetop Method

1. In a large pot, heat oil over medium heat. Cook onion, celery, garlic, cumin, oregano, coriander and cayenne pepper, stirring, for 3 to 4 minutes, until onion and celery are softened. Stir in potatoes, salt and stock; bring to a boil.

2. Cover, reduce heat to low and simmer, stirring occasionally, for about 15 minutes or until potatoes are tender.

3. Meanwhile, in a small saucepan over medium heat, melt butter. Whisk in flour; cook, whisking, for 1 to 2 minutes. (Do not let brown.) Gradually pour in cream while whisking. Remove from heat.

4. To Serve: Remove soup from heat. Uncover pot. Mash with a potato masher a few times to desired consistency. Add cream mixture and cheese, stirring until cheese melts. Stir in sour cream and cumin; season with salt and black pepper to taste.

5. Ladle soup into bowls. Serve topped with thinly sliced Adobo Rubbed Steak, Brad's Incredible Salsa and lime wedges to squeeze over top.

Pressure Cooker Method

1. In a pressure cooker, heat oil over medium heat. Cook onion, celery, garlic, cumin, oregano, coriander and cayenne pepper, stirring, for 3 to 4 minutes, until onion and celery are softened. Stir in potatoes, salt and stock.

2. Lock the pressure lid into place. Heat the pot over high heat and bring pressure to High. Cook for 4 minutes, adjusting heat to maintain pressure as necessary. Remove from heat and let pressure release naturally.

3. Meanwhile, in a small saucepan over medium heat, melt butter. Whisk in flour; cook, whisking, for 1 to 2 minutes. (Do not let brown.) Gradually pour in cream while whisking. Remove from heat.

4. To Serve: Uncover soup pot. Mash with a potato masher a few times to desired consistency. Add cream mixture and cheese, stirring until cheese melts. Stir in sour cream and cumin; season with salt and black pepper to taste.

5. Ladle soup into bowls. Serve topped with thinly sliced Adobo Rubbed Steak, Brad's Incredible Salsa and lime wedges to squeeze over top.

Bread Pairing

Cheddar Corn Jalapeño Muffins (page 75)

Adobo Rubbed Steak

Adobo seasoning gives steak that perfect fajita flavor. Grill over charcoal or on a gas grill or simply sear in a skillet or grill pan. This steak is delicious all by itself but even better as a compliment to Creamy Mexican Potato Soup.

MAKES 8 SERVINGS

- Grill, heavy skillet or grill pan
- Instant-read thermometer

1½ lbs	beef flank or sirloin tip steak	681 g
1 to 2 tsp	adobo seasoning (see Tip, below) or other fajita seasoning blend	6 to 12 g
1 tbsp	olive oil	14 g

1. Sprinkle both sides of steaks with adobo seasoning to taste and drizzle with oil; rub to evenly coat. Let stand at room temperature for up to 30 minutes until ready to cook.

2. Preheat grill, heavy skillet or grill pan over medium-high heat. Cook steak, turning once, until an instant-read thermometer inserted into thickest part of steak reads 145°F (63°C) for medium-rare or to desired doneness. Transfer to a cutting board, tent with foil and let rest for 5 minutes.

3. Cut steak across the grain into thin slices.

Tip

Adobo seasoning, a dried herb and spice blend, is available in the spice section of well-stocked supermarkets, specialty spice stores and online. To make your own, see recipe on page 128.

Creamy Mexican Potato Soup with Adobo Steak and Salsa (page 184) and Cheddar Corn Jalapeño Muffins (page 75)

Brad's Incredible Salsa

My husband, Brad, is known for his incredible salsa, a fresh pico de gallo. We prefer it chunky like pico, but you can mince it as small as you like it. This is his basic recipe, but he will tell you he goes mostly by taste and color, so you may need to adjust the different ingredients a little here and there to best suit your own tastes and heat tolerance.

MAKES ABOUT 4 CUPS (815 G)

5	plum (Roma) tomatoes, finely diced	5
4	sprigs fresh cilantro (approx.), chopped	4
3	cloves garlic, minced	3
1	small onion, finely diced	1
1	yellow, red or green bell pepper, finely diced	1
1	fresh jalapeño pepper, finely diced (optional)	1
	Juice of 2 limes (approx.)	
½ to 1 tsp	salt	3 to 6 g

1. In a bowl, combine tomatoes, cilantro, garlic, onion, bell pepper, jalapeño (if using) and lime juice. Season with salt and more cilantro and lime juice to taste as desired.

16-Bean Soup

16-bean soup mix is a mixture of various beans, lentils and peas. It may vary slightly by brand but it is readily available in most food stores. This hearty soup is very warming and satisfying.

MAKES 8 TO 10 SERVINGS

- Large pot or minimum 6-qt (6 L) pressure cooker

Tips

It's easy to adapt this recipe with your favorite vegetables and seasoning such as celery, green bell peppers, or Cajun spices. As well, a 14- to 15-oz (398 to 425 g) can of diced tomatoes may be added once the beans are done. Stir them in and let simmer a few minutes more to allow the flavors to meld.

To speed up the cooking time for this soup, soak the bean mix using the traditional overnight-soak method, for 6 to 8 hours or overnight, or the pressure cooker quick-soak method on page 29. To cook using the Stovetop Method, in step 3, reduce the cooking time to about 1 hour; for the Pressure Cooker Method, reduce the cooking time to about 20 minutes.

2 tbsp	olive oil	28 g
½ lb	ground beef or turkey	227 g
1	onion, diced	1
2 tbsp	ground cumin	12 g
3	cloves garlic, minced	3
2	medium potatoes, diced	2
1 cup	diced carrots, diced	128 g
1 tsp	dried Italian seasoning	1 g
	Salt and freshly ground black pepper	
	Cayenne pepper	
8 cups	chicken or beef stock or broth (approx.)	1.89 L
2 cups	dry 16-bean soup mix (see Tip, left), rinsed (about 1 lb)	454 g

BEAN SOUP MIX

Bean soup mix is a mixture of beans, peas, legumes and sometimes grains such as barley, combined to make a hearty soup base providing a good number of proteins, carbohydrates and fiber. Depending on the brand, the mixture might have 13, 15, 16 or any number of varieties of beans, peas and legumes to make of the soup mixture. Any of these will work perfectly in this soup.

Stovetop Method

1. In a large pot, heat oil over medium-high heat. Add ground beef and onions; cook, stirring and breaking up meat into chunks, for about 5 minutes, until meat is lightly browned and onions are softened. Add cumin and garlic; cook, stirring, for 1 to 2 minutes or until fragrant.

2. Add potatoes, carrots, Italian seasoning, 1½ tsp (9 g) salt, ½ tsp (1 g) pepper and a pinch of cayenne. Add stock and beans. Make sure beans are covered with about 1 inch (2.5 cm) of liquid; add more stock or water, if needed. Bring soup to a boil, stirring frequently.

3. Cover, reduce heat to low and simmer, stirring occasionally, for about 1½ to 2 hours or until beans are tender.

4. Uncover pot. Season with salt, pepper and cayenne to taste. Ladle soup into bowls.

Pressure Cooker Method

1. In a pressure cooker, heat oil over medium-high heat. Add ground beef and onions; cook, stirring and breaking up meat into chunks, for about 5 minutes, until meat is lightly browned and onions are softened. Add cumin and garlic; cook, stirring, for 1 to 2 minutes or until fragrant.

2. Add potatoes, carrots, Italian seasoning, 1½ tsp (9 g) salt, ½ tsp (1 g) pepper and a pinch of cayenne. Add stock and beans. Make sure beans are covered with about 1 inch (2.5 cm) of liquid; add more stock or water, if needed, being sure not to exceed maximum fill line.

3. Lock the pressure lid into place. Heat the pot over high heat and bring pressure to High. Cook for 45 minutes, adjusting heat as necessary to maintain pressure. Remove from heat and let the pressure release naturally. The beans should be tender. If not, return to pressure and cook in 5-minute increments until done.

4. Uncover pot. Season with salt, pepper and cayenne to taste. Ladle soup into bowls.

Bread Pairing

Peppery Cheese Bread (page 71)

16-Bean Soup (page 188) and
Peppery Cheese Bread (page 71)

Southern-Style Vegetable Soup

This was a staple soup in my home growing up as well as in our first years of marriage when we lived on a tight grocery budget. It was the hardest soup to write into a recipe as it was always made with our home-canned garden tomatoes and green beans and whatever leftovers were in the refrigerator waiting to be used, or better yet in the freezer in a container labeled "for vegetable soup." But here is my best guess — and it was always served with cornbread slathered with butter.

MAKES 6 TO 8 SERVINGS

- Large pot or minimum 6-qt (6 L) pressure cooker

Tips

You can use fresh or frozen soup bones (with some meat on them is best), or bones leftover from a roast beef. Alternatively, for a vegetable soup with beef, you can omit the bones and use $\frac{1}{2}$ to 1 lb (227 to 454 g) beef stew meat, cut into bite-size pieces and cook as directed, until the beef is fork tender.

Use the can of tomato sauce if the soup looks like it needs more liquid when you get everything else into the pot, or you can leave it out for a thick soup.

The ingredients can be adjusted to what you have on hand or to your taste. It's quite flexible, so don't worry about precision in the amounts. You may also add other vegetables like lima beans or okra. I personally do not like okra in my soup because of the gelatinous texture it lends to the broth.

1 tbsp	olive oil	14 g
1	large onion, chopped	1
1 or 2	large meaty beef soup bones (see Tip, left)	1 or 2
2	cans (each 28 oz / 796 g) crushed tomatoes	2
1	can (14 to 15 oz / 398 to 425 g) tomato sauce, optional (see Tip, left)	1
2 or 3	potatoes, diced	2 or 3
2 or 3	large carrots, sliced	2 or 3
1	can (14.5 oz / 411 g) cut green beans, drained (or 1 cup / 135 g frozen)	1
1 cup	whole kernel corn	135 g
	Salt and freshly ground black pepper	

Stovetop Method

1. In a large pot, heat oil over medium heat. Add onion and cook, stirring, for about 5 minutes, until softened. Add beef bones. Cook, turning, until brown on all sides. Add tomatoes, potatoes, carrots, green beans, corn, 1 tbsp (18 g) salt and pepper to taste. Stir well and bring to a boil over high heat.

2. Cover, reduce heat to low simmer, stirring occasionally, for at least 1 hour until vegetables are softened and flavors are blended, or for up to 3 hours, if desired.

3. Uncover pot. Discard bones. Season with salt and pepper to taste. Ladle soup into bowls.

Slow Cooker Variation

This is a perfect soup to dump in a slow cooker and just let it simmer all day. Complete step 1 in the Stovetop Method, then transfer to a minimum 5-qt (5 L) slow cooker. Cover and cook on Low for 8 to 10 hours.

Pressure Cooker Method

1. In a pressure cooker, heat oil over medium heat. Add onion and cook, stirring, for about 5 minutes, until softened. Add beef bones. Cook, turning, until brown on all sides. Add tomatoes, potatoes, carrots, green beans, corn and 1 tbsp (18 g) salt and pepper to taste. Stir well.

2. Lock the pressure lid into place. Heat the pot over high heat and bring pressure to High. Cook for 15 minutes, adjusting heat as necessary to maintain pressure. Remove from heat and let the pressure release naturally. The vegetables should be softened. If not, return to pressure and cook in 2-minute increments until done.

3. Uncover pot. Discard bones. Season with salt and pepper to taste. Ladle soup into bowls.

Bread Pairing

Cornbread (page 68)

Southern-Style Vegetable Soup (page 192)
and Cornbread (page 68)

Leek, Cauliflower and Bacon Chowder

This is a very flavorful, hearty chowder yet completely dairy free. Regular milk may be substituted for the coconut milk with equally delicious results.

MAKES 4 TO 6 SERVINGS

- Large pot or minimum 6-qt (6 L) pressure cooker
- Immersion blender or blender

Tips

My family does not eat pork, so this recipe calls for beef or turkey bacon. Beef bacon has more of the taste and flavor of traditional pork bacon, but it is sometimes hard to find. You may certainly use a bacon of your choice.

Several brands of garlic-and-herb seasoning can usually be found in the spice aisle of most grocery stores. Choose one that doesn't contain salt for this recipe. If you can't find the blend or don't have it on hand, substitute with a clove or two more of minced fresh garlic and 1 tbsp (3 g) of dried Italian seasoning.

1 tbsp	olive oil	14 g
6	slices beef or turkey bacon (see Tip, left), cut in ½-inch (1 cm) pieces	6
1	leek (white and light green parts), diced	1
2	stalks celery, diced	2
2	cloves garlic, minced	2
1	head cauliflower, chopped (about 7 cups / 790 g)	1
2 tbsp	garlic-and-herb seasoning (see Tip, left)	24 g
2 tsp	salt	12 g
1 tsp	freshly ground black pepper	2 g
5 cups	vegetable stock or broth	1.18 L
1	can (14 oz / 398 mL) coconut milk	1
	Chopped fresh parsley	

Stovetop Method

1. In a large pot, heat oil over medium-high heat. Add bacon and cook, stirring, for about 10 minutes or until browned and crisp. Using a slotted spoon, transfer to a paper towel to drain and cool. Set aside.

2. Return pot with oil to medium-high heat. Add leeks and celery; cook, stirring, for about 5 to 6 minutes or until softened. Add garlic and cook, stirring, for 1 minute, until fragrant. Add cauliflower; cook, stirring often, for 5 minutes.

3. Stir in garlic-and-herb seasoning, salt, pepper and stock. Bring to a boil. Cover, reduce heat to low and simmer, stirring occasionally, for 15 to 20 minutes, until cauliflower is soft. Remove from heat.

4. Uncover pot. Stir in coconut milk. Using an immersion blender in the pot, purée until smooth (or transfer the soup to a blender in batches to purée, then return to pot). Return soup to medium heat and bring to a simmer, stirring occasionally.

5. Ladle soup into bowls and sprinkle with reserved bacon and parsley.

Pressure Cooker Method

1. In a pressure cooker, heat oil over medium-high heat. Add bacon and cook, stirring, for about 10 minutes or until browned and crisp. Using a slotted spoon, transfer to a paper towel to drain and cool. Set aside.

2. Return pot with oil to medium-high heat. Add leeks and celery; cook, stirring, for about 5 to 6 minutes or until softened. Add garlic and cook, stirring, for 1 minute, until fragrant. Add cauliflower; cook, stirring often, for 5 minutes.

3. Stir in garlic-and-herb seasoning, salt, pepper and stock. Lock the pressure lid into place. Heat the pot over high heat and bring pressure to High. Cook for 3 minutes, adjusting heat as necessary to maintain pressure. Remove from heat and let pressure release naturally.

4. Uncover pot. Stir in coconut milk. Using an immersion blender in the pot, purée until smooth (or transfer the soup to a blender in batches to purée, then return to pot). Return soup to medium heat and bring to a simmer, stirring occasionally.

5. Ladle soup into bowls and sprinkle with reserved bacon and parsley.

Bread Pairing

Crusty No-Knead Sourdough Bread (page 52)

Leek, Cauliflower and Bacon Chowder (page 196)
and Crusty No-Knead Sourdough Bread (page 52)

Classic Loaded Potato Soup (page 200) and Cheddar Corn Jalapeño Muffins (page 75)

Tuscan Tomato White Bean Soup

This hearty soup is almost a meal in itself. A good piece of fresh-baked, warm bread will complete it.

MAKES 4 TO 6 SERVINGS

- Large pot
- Small skillet
- Baking sheet
- Immersion blender or blender

Tips

If a 7-oz (200 g) jar of tomato paste is not available, use $\frac{3}{4}$ cup (or 200 g) measured from two smaller cans or one larger can.

The metric weights have been calculated as precise conversions from imperial volumes. For ease, you can round the quantities up or down slightly in this soup and still get good results.

1 tbsp	extra virgin olive oil	14 g
1	large onion, chopped	1
3	cloves garlic, minced	1
	Salt	
1	jar (7 oz / 200 g) tomato paste (see Tip, left)	1
2 lbs	tomatoes, chopped, divided	908 g
3 cups	drained cooked cannellini (white kidney) beans (or two 14- to 15-oz / 398 to 425 g cans, drained and rinsed)	540 g
4 cups	vegetable or chicken stock or broth	944 mL
1 cup	water	236 mL
1	sprig fresh rosemary	1
	Red pepper flakes	
	Freshly ground black pepper	
	Extra virgin olive oil	

CROUTONS

4 cups	cubed Ciabatta Bread (page 62) or other hearty bread	240 g
2 tbsp	extra virgin olive oil	28 g
2	cloves garlic, minced	2
1 tsp	chopped fresh rosemary leaves	2 g
$\frac{1}{2}$ cup	shredded mozzarella cheese	56 g
Pinch	salt	Pinch
	Red pepper flakes	

Stovetop Method

1. In a large pot, heat olive oil over medium-high heat. Add onion, garlic and a pinch of salt; cook, stirring occasionally, for 5 minutes or until onion is softened. Add tomato paste; cook, stirring, for 1 minute.

2. Reserve ½ cup (90 g) of the chopped tomatoes for garnish. Add remaining tomatoes, beans, stock, water, rosemary sprig, ½ tsp (3 g) salt and ¼ tsp (0.5 g) red pepper flakes to the pot. Bring to a boil. Reduce heat to medium and simmer, stirring occasionally, for about 20 minutes or until tomatoes are soft and flavors are blended. Remove from heat.

3. Croutons: Meanwhile, preheat oven to 400°F (200°C). Place bread cubes in a large bowl.

4. In a small skillet, heat olive oil and garlic over medium heat. Cook, stirring occasionally, for about 2 minutes, until lightly browned, being careful not to burn. Pour over bread cubes in bowl; add rosemary, mozzarella and salt, tossing to evenly coat. Spread on baking sheet. Sprinkle with red pepper flakes to taste. Bake, stirring occasionally, for about 10 minutes or until croutons are golden brown. Set aside.

5. To finish soup, discard rosemary sprig. Using an immersion blender in the pot, pulse until soup is desired consistency, leaving some beans whole (or transfer the soup to a blender in batches and purée about half of the soup, then return to pot). Return soup to medium-low heat and return to a simmer, if necessary. Season with salt, pepper and red pepper flakes to taste, if desired.

6. Ladle soup into bowls and top with croutons and reserved chopped tomatoes. Drizzle with olive oil.

Bread Pairing

Ciabatta Bread (page 62)

Tuscan Tomato White Bean Soup (page 204) and Ciabatta Bread (page 62)

Black Bean Soup

A longtime friend shared this recipe with me years ago. I love the unique hint of flavors of cloves and orange in this soup. It is delicious served over cooked brown rice or cooked hulled barley.

MAKES 8 TO 10 SERVINGS

- Large pot or minimum 6-qt (6 L) pressure cooker

Tip

The metric weights have been calculated as precise conversions from imperial volumes. For ease, you can round the quantities up or down slightly in this soup and still get good results. For small amounts of spices and herbs, measuring spoons are easiest.

2 tbsp	olive oil	28 g
1	large onion, diced	1
3	cloves garlic, minced	3
1½ tsp	salt	9 g
1 tsp	ground cumin	2 g
½ tsp	freshly ground black pepper	1 g
½ tsp	dried oregano leaves	0.5 g
½ tsp	ground cloves	1 g
¼ tsp	dried thyme leaves	0.25 g
¼ tsp	dry mustard	0.5 g
Pinch	cayenne pepper	Pinch
2	bay leaves	2
2 cups	dry black beans, rinsed	400 g
5 to 6 cups	water	1.18 to 1.42 L
	Juice of 1 orange	
	Additional olive oil	

OVERNIGHT-SOAK METHOD

To speed up the cooking time for this soup, soak the beans using the traditional overnight-soak method, for 6 to 8 hours or overnight, or the pressure cooker quick-soak method on page 29. To cook using the stovetop method, in step 3, reduce the cooking time to about 1 hour; for the pressure cooker method, reduce the cooking time to about 20 minutes.

Stovetop Method

1. In a large pot, heat oil over medium-high heat. Add onion and cook, stirring, for about 5 minutes or until softened. Add garlic, salt, cumin, pepper, oregano, cloves, thyme, mustard, cayenne and bay leaves; cook, stirring, for 1 to 2 minutes, until fragrant. Add beans and enough water to cover by 1 inch (2.5 cm). Bring to a boil over high heat.

2. Cover, reduce heat to low and simmer, stirring occasionally, for 1½ to 2 hours if beans or until beans are tender.

3. Uncover pot. Discard bay leaves. Stir in orange juice. Ladle into bowls and garnish with a drizzle of olive oil to taste.

Pressure Cooker Method

1. In a pressure cooker, heat oil over medium-high heat. Add onion and cook, stirring, for about 5 minutes or until softened. Add garlic, salt, cumin, pepper, oregano, cloves, thyme, mustard, cayenne and bay leaves; cook, stirring, for 1 to 2 minutes, until fragrant. Add beans and enough water to cover by 1 inch (2.5 cm), being sure not to exceed maximum fill line.

2. Lock the pressure lid into place. Heat the pot over high heat and bring pressure to High. Cook for 45 minutes, adjusting heat as necessary to maintain pressure. Remove from heat and let the pressure release naturally. The beans should be tender. If not, return to pressure and cook in 5-minute increments until done.

3. Uncover pot. Discard bay leaves. Stir in orange juice. Ladle into bowls and garnish with a drizzle of olive oil to taste.

Bread Pairing

Authentic Pan Pita (page 65)

Black Bean Soup (page 208) and
Authentic Pan Pita (page 65)

Broccoli Cheddar Soup

The added potatoes and sweet potatoes to this classic soup gives it a creamy texture and vibrant color, making it one of my favorite soups. Cooked using a pressure cooker, this soup is ready in less than 30 minutes.

MAKES 8 TO 10 SERVINGS

- Large pot or minimum 6-qt (6 L) pressure cooker
- Large saucepan
- Immersion blender or blender

Tips

The metric weights have been calculated as precise conversions from imperial volumes. For ease, you can round the quantities up or down slightly in this soup and still get good results.

When puréeing hot soup in a regular blender, be sure not to fill more than half-full to prevent splashing and slightly open the filler cap (which covers the hole in the lid) to let steam escape while blending. For extra safety, you may want to hold a tea towel over the lid as well.

2 tbsp	olive oil	28 g
1	onion, finely chopped	1
4	stalks celery, finely chopped	4
4 cups	vegetable or chicken stock or broth	944 mL
2 lbs	potatoes, peeled and cubed	908 g
2 lbs	sweet potatoes, peeled and cubed	908 g
2	bay leaves	2
2 tsp	salt	12 g
½ tsp	freshly ground black pepper	1 g
4 cups	water	944 mL
4 cups	broccoli florets	360 g
4 cups	half-and-half (10%) cream	944 mL
1 lb	sharp (aged) Cheddar cheese or smoked Cheddar cheese	454 g
	Spicy Cajun Croutons (optional, recipe page 214)	

Stovetop Method

1. In a large pot, heat oil over medium heat. Add onion and celery; cook, stirring, for about 3 minutes, until softened. Add stock, potatoes, sweet potatoes, bay leaves, 2 tsp (12 g) salt, ½ tsp (1 g) pepper and water. Bring to a boil over high heat. Cover, reduce heat to low and simmer for about 20 minutes or until potatoes are soft.

2. Meanwhile, place about 1 inch (2.5 cm) of water in a large saucepan. Add broccoli and bring to a boil over high heat. Cover and remove from heat to let broccoli steam naturally, about 10 minutes.

3. Uncover soup and discard bay leaves. Using an immersion blender in the pot, purée until smooth (or transfer the soup to a blender in batches to purée, then return to pot).

4. Return soup to medium-low heat and return to a simmer, stirring occasionally. Stir in steamed broccoli with any accumulated liquid and cream. Add cheese and stir until melted. Season with salt and pepper to taste.

5. Ladle soup into bowls and top with Spicy Cajun Croutons, if desired.

Pressure Cooker Method

1. In a pressure cooker, heat oil over medium heat. Add onion and celery; cook, stirring, for about 3 minutes, until softened. Add stock, potatoes, sweet potatoes, bay leaves, 2 tsp (12 g) salt, ½ tsp (1 g) pepper and water. Lock the pressure lid into place. Heat the pot over high heat and bring pressure to High. Cook for 3 minutes, adjusting heat as necessary to maintain pressure. Remove from heat and quick-release the pressure.

2. Meanwhile, place about 1 inch (2.5 cm) of water in a large saucepan. Add broccoli and bring to a boil over high heat. Cover and remove from heat to let broccoli steam naturally, about 10 minutes.

3. Uncover soup pot and discard bay leaves. Using an immersion blender in the pot, purée until smooth (or transfer the soup to a blender in batches to purée, then return to pot).

4. Return soup to medium-low heat and return to a simmer. Stir in steamed broccoli with any accumulated liquid and cream. Add cheese and stir until melted. Season with salt and pepper to taste.

5. Ladle soup into bowls and top with Spicy Cajun Croutons, if desired.

Bread Pairing

Mushroom Cheese Bread (page 44)

Spicy Cajun Croutons

We love the bold flavor these croutons add to our bowl of soup or Caesar salad. Feel free to change the seasoning to suit your tastes, for example, substituting 2 tsp (2 g) dried Italian seasoning for the Cajun.

MAKES ABOUT 4 CUPS (250 G)

Preheat oven to 400°F (200°C)

- Baking sheet

3 tbsp	olive oil	42 g
2 tsp	Cajun seasoning	12 g
2	cloves garlic, minced	2
4 cups	day-old bread cubes ($\frac{3}{4}$-inch / 2 cm pieces), such as Basic Yeast Bread (page 34) or other hearty bread	240 g

1. In a large bowl, whisk together olive oil, Cajun seasoning and garlic. Add bread cubes and toss until well coated. Spread in a single layer on baking sheet.

2. Bake in preheated oven for 10 minutes. Stir and bake for 5 minutes, until golden brown and crisp, being careful not to let burn. Let cool completely. Croutons can be stored in an airtight container for up to 1 week.

Broccoli Cheddar Soup (page 212)
with Spicy Cajun Croutons

Cream of Tomato Basil Soup

This is a very easy soup to put together and is especially good in the summer when fresh tomatoes are available. I first tasted this soup for lunch at a good friend's house and requested the recipe. When I serve it, most people say it's the best tomato soup they have had. Growing up, my favorite lunch, especially if I was home sick from school, was tomato soup with a grilled cheese sandwich. My new favorite is Grilled Pimento Cheese. (I didn't know Pimento Cheese was a "Southern thing.")

MAKES 4 TO 6 SERVINGS

- Large pot or minimum 5-qt (5 L) pressure cooker
- Immersion blender or blender

Tips

The metric weights have been calculated as precise conversions from imperial volumes. For ease, you can round the quantities up or down slightly in this soup and still get good results.

If tomatoes are not very flavorful, you might want to add the tomato paste for a richer tasting soup.

You can use any type of wheat or bean flour to thicken the soup. Use an equal volume of other flours; if measuring by weight, see the chart on page 24 to calculate the weight for 3 tbsp of the flour you're using.

1⁄3 cup	unsalted butter	76 g
1 tbsp	olive oil	14 g
1 cup	chopped onion	130 g
1 1⁄2 lbs	fresh tomatoes, coarsely chopped (or one 28-oz / 796 g can diced tomatoes)	681 g
1⁄2 tsp	dried basil leaves	0.5 g
1⁄4 tsp	dried thyme leaves	0.25 g
	Freshly ground black pepper	
3 tbsp	freshly milled soft wheat flour	24 g
2 cups	vegetable or chicken stock or broth, divided	472 g
1⁄4 cup	tomato paste (optional, see Tip, left)	64 g
1⁄4 tsp	baking soda	2 g
1⁄2 tsp	honey granules or granulated cane sugar (optional)	2 g
1⁄2 cup	heavy or whipping (35%) cream or whole milk	120 g
	Salt	

Stovetop Method

1. In a large pot, melt butter and heat oil over medium-high heat. Add onion and cook, stirring, for about 5 minutes, until tender. Add tomatoes, basil, thyme and pepper to taste. Bring to a simmer. Cover, reduce heat to low and simmer for about 10 minutes or until tomatoes are soft.

2. In a small bowl, whisk together flour with ½ cup (118 g) of the stock until smooth.

3. Uncover pot. Gradually pour in flour mixture, stirring constantly. Stir in the remaining stock and tomato paste (if using). Cover and simmer over low heat, stirring occasionally, for about 25 minutes, to blend the flavors. Remove from heat.

4. Using an immersion blender in the pot, purée until smooth (or transfer the soup to a blender in batches to purée, then return to pot). Add baking soda; blend thoroughly; if using a blender, add with last batch and stir well when returning to the pot.

5. Return soup to medium-low heat. Stir in the honey granules (if using) and cream. Heat, stirring occasionally, until steaming (do not let boil). Season with salt to taste. Ladle into bowls.

Pressure Cooker Method

1. In a pressure cooker, melt butter and heat oil over medium-high heat. Add onion and cook, stirring, for about 5 minutes, until tender. Add tomatoes, basil, thyme and pepper to taste. Lock the pressure lid into place. Heat the pot over high heat and bring pressure to High. Cook for 3 minutes, adjusting heat as necessary to maintain pressure. Remove from heat and let pressure release naturally.

2. In a small bowl, whisk together flour with ½ cup (118 g) of the stock until smooth.

3. Uncover pot. Gradually pour in flour mixture, stirring constantly. Stir in the remaining stock and tomato paste (if using). Cover and simmer over low heat for about 25 minutes, to blend the flavors. Remove from heat.

4. Using an immersion blender in the pot, purée until smooth (or transfer the soup to a blender in batches to purée, then return to pot). Add baking soda; blend thoroughly; if using a blender, add with last batch and stir well when returning to the pot.

5. Return soup to medium-low heat. Stir in the honey granules (if using) and cream. Heat, stirring occasionally, until steaming (do not let boil). Season with salt to taste. Ladle into bowls.

Bread Pairing

Grilled Pimento Cheese Sandwiches (page 46)

Cream of Tomato Basil Soup (page 216) and Grilled Pimento Cheese Sandwiches (page 46)

Sweet Potato Bisque (page 220) with
Basic Yeast Bread Loaf and Sandwich Rolls (page 34)

Leek and Potato Soup
with Green Onion Purée and Garlic-Herb Cheese Croutons

This soup was inspired by my good friend, Judith McLoughlin, a professional chef, "fresh off the boat," as she says, from Northern Ireland. Judith and her husband, Gary, settled in Georgia near where I live. She partnered with me to teach an Irish cooking class, and this was a favorite dish served. I am blessed to call her my friend.

MAKES 4 TO 6 SERVINGS

- Large pot
- Small pot and small saucepan
- Immersion blender or blender
- Baking sheet, ungreased

Tips

Judith likes to use Irish butter for this recipe. Known for its exceptional taste and creamy texture, Irish butter comes to us thanks to pasture-raised cows in that lush green land and is available in larger grocery stores this side of the Atlantic. If it's not available, any good salted butter can be used.

Dubliner cheese is a delicious semi-hard Irish cheese originating in Dublin, Ireland, but readily available in most grocery stores. It has the taste of sharp Cheddar and the firmness of Parmesan. If it's not available, a good Parmesan, Gouda, Gruyère or a combination of these may be substituted.

Preheat oven to 325°F (160°F)

SOUP

½ cup	salted butter (see Tip, left)	118 g
1	onion, diced	1
2	large leeks (white part and light green parts), sliced	2
5	potatoes (about 4 cups / 520 g), peeled and diced	5
4 cups	vegetable or chicken stock or broth	944 mL
1 tsp	salt (approx.)	6 g
	Freshly ground black pepper	
2 tbsp	heavy or whipping (35%) cream	30 g

GARLIC-HERB CHEESE CROUTONS

2 cups	day-old bread cubes (½-inch / 1 cm pieces)	120 g
¼ cup	garlic-and-herb butter	57 g
¼ cup	finely shredded Dubliner cheese (see Tip, left)	28 g

GREEN ONION PURÉE

	Salt	
4	green onions, coarsely chopped	4
	Ice water	
¼ cup	salted butter, melted	57 g

Stovetop Method

1. In a large pot, melt butter over low heat. Cook onion and leeks, stirring occasionally allowing them to "sweat" without browning, for about 15 minutes, until softened and fragrant. Add potatoes, stock, 1 tsp (6 g) salt and pepper, to taste. Bring to a boil over medium heat.

2. Cover, reduce heat to low and gently simmer for about 20 to 25 minutes or until potatoes are soft. Remove from heat.

3. Using an immersion blender in the pot, purée until smooth (or transfer the soup to a blender in batches to purée, then return to pot). Cover to keep warm while making croutons and green onion purée.

4. Garlic-Herb Cheese Croutons: Place bread cubes in a large bowl. In a small saucepan, melt garlic-and-herb butter over low heat. Pour over bread cubes and toss to coat. Spread out in a single layer on a baking sheet.

5. Bake in preheated oven for 10 to 15 minutes, turning halfway through, until crunchy and toasted. Sprinkle cheese over croutons and bake for 1 minute, until melted. Let cool.

6. Green Onion Purée: Meanwhile, in a small pot of boiling, salted water, blanch green onions for just under 1 minute. Drain immediately and place in a bowl of ice water to stop the cooking.

7. In a small saucepan, melt butter over low heat; remove from heat. Drain green onions and transfer to a tall cup to use an immersion blender, or to a blender; purée until smooth. With the motor running, slowly drizzle in the melted butter until blended and frothy (drizzle through the hole in blender lid, if using).

8. To serve, return soup to medium heat and bring to a simmer, stirring occasionally. Reduce heat to low and stir in cream. Season with salt and pepper, to taste.

9. Ladle soup into bowls with a drizzle of the frothy Green Onion Purée and Garlic-Herb Cheese Croutons.

Pressure Cooker Variation

While Judith doesn't use a pressure cooker to make this soup, you certainly can do so for step 2. Lock the pressure lid into place. Heat the pot over high heat and bring pressure to High. Cook for 5 minutes, adjusting heat as necessary to maintain pressure. Remove from heat and let pressure release naturally.

Bread Pairing

Cheddar and Herb Crusty No-Knead Bread (page 51) or Crusty No-Knead Bread (page 48)

Leek and Potato Soup with Green Onion Purée and Garlic-Herb Cheese Croutons (page 224) and Crusty No-Knead Bread (page 48)

Curried Lentil Soup

I developed this recipe to replicate a prepared soup that I loved but was discontinued. I had to find a way to make it. This version is very close and equally delicious. You can also garnish each bowl with my Spicy Cajun Croutons (page 214) or your favorite homemade croutons.

MAKES 4 TO 6 SERVINGS

- Large pot or minimum 5-qt (5 L) pressure cooker
- Immersion blender or blender

Tip

The metric weights have been calculated as precise conversions from imperial volumes. For ease, you can round the quantities up or down slightly in this soup and still get good results.

2 tsp	olive oil	10 g
Half	onion, chopped	Half
1 tbsp	grated fresh gingerroot	13 g
1 tbsp	curry powder	7 g
2 cups	baby carrots (or 4 medium carrots, diced)	250 g
1	apple, peeled and chopped	1
$\frac{3}{4}$ cup	dried red lentils	135 g
4 cups	vegetable stock or broth	944 mL
	Salt and freshly ground black pepper	
1 tbsp	ground turmeric	7 g
	Red pepper flakes	

ABOUT RED LENTILS

Dried red lentils are small and more tender than larger brown or green lentils and don't need to be soaked before cooking. Do pick through to remove any husks or stones or discolored ones. If they are very dusty you may want to give them a rinse in a sieve before using to avoid a gluey texture.

Stovetop Method

1. In a large pot, heat oil over medium-high heat. Cook onion, stirring, for about 5 minutes, until translucent. Add ginger and curry powder; cook, stirring, for 30 seconds, until fragrant. Stir in carrots, apple, lentils, stock, 1 tsp (6 g) salt and $\frac{1}{4}$ tsp (0.5 g) pepper. Bring to a boil over high heat.

2. Cover, reduce heat to low and simmer, stirring occasionally, for about 30 to 45 minutes or until carrots and lentils are soft. Remove from heat.

3. Uncover pot. Using an immersion blender in the pot, purée until smooth (or transfer the soup to a blender in batches to purée, then return to pot).

4. Return soup to medium heat. Stir in turmeric. Season with red pepper flakes, salt and pepper to taste. Reheat until steaming, stirring occasionally. Ladle into bowls.

Pressure Cooker Method

1. In a pressure cooker, heat oil over medium-high heat. Cook onion, stirring, for about 5 minutes, until translucent. Add ginger and curry powder; cook, stirring, for 30 seconds, until fragrant. Stir in carrots, apple, lentils, stock, 1 tsp (6 g) salt and $\frac{1}{4}$ tsp (0.5 g) pepper.

2. Lock the pressure lid into place. Heat the pot over high heat and bring pressure to High. Cook for 10 minutes, adjusting heat as necessary to maintain pressure. Remove from heat and let pressure release naturally or quick-release the pressure.

3. Uncover pot. Using an immersion blender in the pot, purée until smooth (or transfer the soup to a blender in batches to purée, then return to pot).

4. Return soup to medium heat. Stir in turmeric. Season with red pepper flakes, salt and pepper to taste. Reheat until steaming, stirring occasionally. Ladle into bowls.

Bread Pairing

Indian Naan (page 66)

Curried Lentil Soup (page 228)
and Indian Naan (page 66)

Cream of Mushroom Soup

Any variety of mushrooms may be used to make this creamy, savory soup. To satisfy all your mushroom cravings, serve it with the savory Mushroom Cheese Bread.

MAKES 4 TO 6 SERVINGS

- Large pot
- Immersion blender or blender

1/4 cup	unsalted butter, divided	57 g
1 tbsp	olive oil	14 g
3/4 tsp	cumin seeds (or 1/2 tsp / 1 g ground cumin)	2 g
1 lb	mixed mushrooms, coarsely chopped	454 g
1/2 cup	brown ale or dark amber beer	118 g
3	leeks (white and light green parts), thinly sliced	3
2	cloves garlic, chopped	2
4 cups	vegetable or chicken stock or broth	944 mL
1 tsp	salt	6 g
1/2 tsp	freshly ground black pepper	1 g
1/4 cup	heavy or whipping (35%) cream	60 g

CHOOSE YOUR FAVORITE MUSHROOM FLAVOR

Believe it or not, white button, baby bella and even portabello mushrooms are all the same variety of mushrooms. What makes them different is how long they are left to mature before cultivating, which affects both their flavor and texture.

White button mushrooms are the youngest and therefore more tender and milder in flavor. They are perfect for eating raw, using whole in sauce or soups, and for marinating.

Baby bellas, also called crimini, cremini and brown mushrooms, are slightly more mature, with a nice brown color and deeper earthy flavor.

Portabello mushrooms are the most mature of the three, which gives them an even deeper earthy flavor as well as a firmer, drier texture, making them the best choice for grilling or roasting.

Stovetop Method

1. In a large pot, melt 2 tbsp (28 g) of the butter and heat oil over medium-high heat. Add cumin seeds and cook, stirring, for 1 to 2 minutes, until fragrant and lightly toasted. Add mushrooms and cook, stirring occasionally, for about 8 minutes, until liquid is evaporated and mushrooms are golden brown. Transfer a heaping spoonful of the mushrooms to a bowl for garnish, if desired; set aside.

2. Add ale to the pot; cook, stirring often, for 1 to 2 minutes or until liquid is evaporated. Add remaining butter and leeks; cook, stirring occasionally, for about 5 minutes, until tender. Add garlic; cook, stirring, for 1 minute, until fragrant. Add stock, 1 tsp (6 g) salt and ¼ tsp (0.5 g) pepper to pot. Stir well, scraping up any browned bits from the bottom of the pot.

3. Remove from heat. Using an immersion blender in the pot, purée until smooth (or transfer the soup to a blender in batches to purée, then return to pot).

4. Return soup to medium heat. Stir in cream and bring to a simmer, stirring occasionally. Season to taste with salt and pepper.

5. Ladle into bowls and garnish with reserved mushrooms, if desired.

Bread Pairing

Mushroom Cheese Bread (page 44)

Cream of Mushroom Soup (page 232)
and Mushroom Cheese Bread (page 44)

Creamy Mushroom, Garlic and Rice Soup

This rich and creamy soup will thicken as it cools to an almost risotto texture, so leftovers can easily be served as a side dish.

MAKES 6 TO 8 SERVINGS

- Large skillet
- Large pot
- Food processor or blender

Tip

You'll need to cook 1 cup (200 g) whole-grain brown rice to get 3 cups (560 g) cooked for this recipe. See the Classic Chicken and Brown Rice Soup (page 97) for stovetop and pressure cooker directions.

2 tbsp	unsalted butter	28 g
3 tbsp	olive oil	42 g
1 lb	white mushrooms, sliced	454 g
1	large sweet onion, finely chopped	1
3	cloves garlic, minced	3
8 oz	block-style cream cheese, softened and cubed	227 g
2 tbsp	dried Italian seasoning	6 g
3 cups	cooked brown rice, divided (see Tip, left)	560 g
4 cups	vegetable or chicken stock or broth, divided	944 mL
2 cups	water or additional stock or broth, optional	472 mL
2 tsp	salt	12 g
	Freshly ground black pepper	

TOPPINGS, OPTIONAL

	Chopped fresh chives or green onions	
	Olive oil	

Stovetop Method

1. In large skillet, melt butter and heat oil over medium-high heat. Add mushrooms and onion; cook, stirring occasionally, for about 10 minutes or until onions are softened, liquid is evaporated and mushrooms are golden brown. Add garlic and cook, stirring, for 1 minute, until fragrant. Remove from heat and let cool slightly. Transfer a heaping spoonful of the mushroom mixture to a bowl for garnish, if desired; set aside.

2. In a food processor or blender, combine cream cheese and Italian seasoning; process until blended and fairly smooth. Add remaining mushroom mixture, 1½ cups (280 g) of the cooked rice and 1 cup (236 mL) of the broth. Pulse mixture until mushrooms are finely chopped but not puréed and mixture is thoroughly combined. (If you don't have a large food processor or blender, do this in two batches for easier blending.)

3. Transfer mushroom mixture to a large pot. Stir in remaining rice, stock and water or additional stock, as necessary, to thin to desired thickness. Stir in salt and pepper to taste. Bring to a simmer over medium-high heat, stirring occasionally. Reduce heat to low and simmer, uncovered, for about 5 minutes to blend the flavors.

4. Ladle soup into bowls and garnish with reserved sautéed mushrooms, chives and a drizzle of olive oil, if desired.

Bread Pairing

Easy Drop Biscuits (page 76)

Creamy Mushroom, Garlic and Rice Soup (page 236)
and Easy Drop Biscuits (page 76)

Creamy Butternut Squash Bisque
with Caramelized Onions and Croutons

The term "bisque" originally referred to a fish-based creamy soup. Today, bisque can be any smooth and creamy soup focused on one main ingredient. This dish certainly qualifies, with butternut squash as the star. Its flavor, sweetness and creaminess are enhanced by a few additional ingredients. To add a savory touch, serve topped with sweet Caramelized Onions and croutons.

MAKES 6 SERVINGS

- Large pot or minimum 5-qt (5 L) pressure cooker
- Medium skillet
- Immersion blender or blender

Tips

The metric weights have been calculated as precise conversions from imperial volumes. For ease, you can round the quantities up or down slightly in this soup and still get good results.

The Caramelized Onions can be made ahead. Cook as directed in step 3 and let cool completely. Store in an airtight container in the refrigerator for up to 5 days. Warm slightly in a saucepan over medium-low heat before serving. Extra caramelized onions can be used on pizzas or sandwiches.

1⁄4 cup	unsalted butter	57 g
1	large onion, chopped	1
	Salt	
2 tbsp	tomato paste	32 g
2 lbs	butternut squash, peeled, seeded and cut into chunks	908 g
4 cups	vegetable or chicken stock or broth	944 mL
	Red pepper flakes	
1⁄2 cup	heavy or whipping (35%) cream	120 g
2 tbsp	pure maple syrup	30 g
	Cracked black pepper	

CARAMELIZED ONIONS

2 tbsp	unsalted butter	28 g
1	large onion, very thinly sliced	1
2	cloves garlic, minced	2
1 1⁄2 tbsp	dark unrefined cane sugar or brown sugar	15 g
1⁄2 tsp	salt	3 g
2 tsp	Worcestershire sauce	10 g
	Spicy Cajun Croutons made with Italian seasoning (page 214)	

Stovetop Method

1. In a large pot, melt butter over medium heat. Add onion and 1 tsp (6 g) salt; cook, stirring, about 5 minutes until onion is softened. Add tomato paste; cook, stirring, for about 2 minutes, until the onions just begin to turn golden.

2. Add squash, stock, 1 tsp (6 g) salt and a pinch of red pepper flakes. Bring to a boil. Cover, reduce heat to low and simmer, stirring occasionally, for about 25 minutes or until squash is very tender. Remove soup from heat.

3. **Caramelized Onions:** Meanwhile, in a skillet, melt butter over medium-high heat. Add onion and cook, stirring frequently, for 3 to 4 minutes or until tender. Add garlic, sugar, salt and Worcestershire sauce; cook, stirring frequently, for 5 to 10 minutes until onions are browned and tender. Remove from heat and set aside.

4. Uncover soup pot. Using an immersion blender in the pot, purée until smooth (or transfer the soup to a blender in batches to purée, then return to pot).

5. Return soup to low heat. Bring to a gentle simmer, stirring occasionally. Stir in cream and maple syrup. Season with salt and pepper to taste.

6. Ladle soup into bowls. Garnish with Caramelized Onions, Spicy Cajun Croutons and more red pepper flakes, if desired.

Pressure Cooker Method

1. In a pressure cooker, melt butter over medium heat. Add onion and 1 tsp (6 g) salt; cook, stirring, about 5 minutes until onion is softened. Add tomato paste; cook, stirring, for about 2 minutes, until the onions just begin to turn golden.

2. Add squash, stock, 1 tsp (6 g) salt and a pinch of red pepper flakes. Lock the pressure lid into place. Heat the pot over high heat and bring pressure to High. Cook for 5 minutes, adjusting heat as necessary to maintain pressure. Remove from heat and let pressure release naturally

3. **Caramelized Onions:** Meanwhile, in a skillet, melt butter over medium-high heat. Add onion and cook, stirring frequently, for 3 to 4 minutes or until tender. Add garlic, sugar, salt and Worcestershire sauce; cook, stirring frequently, for 5 to 10 minutes until onions are browned and tender. Remove from heat and set aside.

4. Uncover soup pot. Using an immersion blender in the pot, purée until smooth (or transfer the soup to a blender in batches to purée, then return to pot).

5. Return soup to low heat. Bring to a gentle simmer, stirring occasionally. Stir in cream and maple syrup. Season with salt and pepper to taste.

6. Ladle soup into bowls. Garnish with Caramelized Onions, Spicy Cajun Croutons and more red pepper flakes, if desired.

Bread Pairing

Buttermilk Potato Bread (page 61)

Creamy Butternut Squash Bisque with Caramelized Onions and Croutons (page 240) and Buttermilk Potato Bread (page 61)

My Favorite Turkey Chili
with Sweet Potatoes

This may not sound unique, but it's one of the best chilies I've ever had! And it's my go-to recipe when I want chili. Nothing fancy, just delicious. Everyone who tastes it wants the recipe. It's easy to make ahead of time and tastes even better the next day once the flavors and spices have had time to meld.

MAKES 6 TO 8 SERVINGS

- Large pot or minimum 6-qt (6 L) pressure cooker

Tips

Note that for this recipe, I don't drain and rinse the beans in the can — I use all the contents of the can. The liquid in the beans adds a nice, thick texture to the chili.

You can use two cans of the same beans or one can of each.

Instead of buying canned beans, you can easily cook dried beans in the pressure cooker. See page 29 for instructions. For the two cans called for in the recipe, use a total of 3⅓ cups (850 g) cooked beans with liquid. For this recipe, you'll need to soak and cook a total of about 1¼ cups (250 g) dried beans.

This chili can be made ahead and refrigerated for up to 3 days or frozen. See page 31 for detailed instructions.

2 tbsp	olive oil	28 g
1 lb	ground turkey, preferably dark meat	454 g
1	onion, chopped	1
4	cloves garlic, chopped	4
1	jalapeño pepper, seeded and chopped, optional	1
1 tbsp	Mexican chili powder or regular chili powder	18 g
2 tsp	salt	12 g
2 tsp	ground cumin	4 g
Pinch	ground cloves	Pinch
	Freshly ground black pepper	
1	can (28 oz / 796 g) diced tomatoes	1
2	cans (each 14 to 15 oz / 398 to 425 g) dark red kidney or pinto beans, with liquid (see Tip, left)	2
2	small sweet potatoes, peeled and cubed	2

TOPPINGS, OPTIONAL

Sour cream or plain yogurt

Chopped fresh cilantro

Hot sauce

Stovetop Method

1. In a large pot, heat oil over high heat. Add turkey and cook, stirring and breaking up into chunks, until browned. Stir in onion, garlic and jalapeño (if using); cook, stirring, for about 3 minutes, until softened. Stir in chili powder, salt, cumin, cloves and pepper to taste; cook, stirring, for 1 minute, until fragrant.

2. Stir in tomatoes, beans and sweet potatoes; bring to a simmer, stirring occasionally. Cover, reduce heat to low and simmer, stirring occasionally, for about 30 minutes or until sweet potatoes are very soft, and mash and blend into sauce with stirring.

3. Ladle chili into bowls and serve topped with sour cream, cilantro and hot sauce, as desired.

Slow Cooker Variation

To cook this chili in the slow cooker, follow the Stovetop Method through the addition of tomatoes, beans and sweet potatoes in step 2, then transfer to a minimum 5-qt (5 L) slow cooker. Cover and cook on Low for 6 to 8 hours.

Pressure Cooker Method

1. In a pressure cooker, heat oil over high heat. Add turkey and cook, stirring and breaking up into chunks, until browned. Stir in onion, garlic and jalapeño (if using); cook, stirring, for about 3 minutes, until softened. Stir in chili powder, salt, cumin, cloves and pepper to taste; cook, stirring, for 1 minute, until fragrant.

2. Stir in tomatoes, beans and sweet potatoes. Lock the pressure lid into place. Heat the pot over high heat and bring pressure to High. Cook for 5 minutes, adjusting heat to maintain pressure as necessary. Remove from heat and let the pressure release naturally.

3. Ladle chili into bowls and serve topped with sour cream, cilantro and hot sauce, as desired.

Bread Pairing

Peppery Cheese Bread (page 71)

My Favorite Turkey Chili with Sweet Potatoes (page 244) and Peppery Cheese Bread (page 71)

Roasted Garlic White Bean Chili (page 248)
and Cheddar-Jalapeño Bread (page 37)

Easy Chicken Ranch Chili

This is a fast and easy chili recipe that can be served as a special treat over waffles or over rice, or simply with tortillas chips for dipping. However you serve it, it can stand alone as a meal. Any way you want to cook it — stovetop, pressure cooker, oven or slow cooker — it is hearty and delicious. And the hands-on prep time is less than 10 minutes.

MAKES 4 TO 6 SERVINGS

- Dutch oven or minimum 4½-qt (4.5 L) pressure cooker, preferably skillet style

Tips

You can use plain diced tomatoes or boost the flavor with fire-roasted tomatoes or any seasoned diced tomatoes.

I prefer to use a ranch dip or seasoning mix that contains no added sugar or MSG.

2	boneless chicken breasts (about 1 lb / 454 g), cut into bite-size pieces	2
1	can (15 oz / 425 g) whole kernel corn	1
1	can (14 to 15 oz / 398 to 425 g) Great Northern or navy beans, drained and rinsed	1
1	can (28 oz / 796 g) diced tomatoes (see Tip, left)	1
2 tbsp	dry ranch or Southwest ranch dip seasoning mix	24 g
2 tsp	chili powder	12 g
8 oz	block-style cream cheese	227 g

CORNBREAD AND CHILI

A hot bowl of chili just screams for cornbread, like my classic Cornbread (page 68) or the Chedder Corn Jalapeño Muffins (page 75).

And then there are cornbread waffles! A few years back, I got the idea of making my regular waffle recipe using freshly milled corn flour, adding some cheese and jalapeño peppers to the batter and cooking them to serve with my chili spooned on top. Add a dollop of sour cream and we had a hit, guaranteed to wow them at any chili cook-off!

Stovetop Method

1. Spread chicken pieces in the bottom of a Dutch oven. Scatter corn and beans over top of chicken; pour tomatoes evenly over. Sprinkle with ranch seasoning and chili powder. Place cream cheese on top.

2. Cover and cook over high heat for about 5 minutes or until liquid is simmering. Reduce heat to low and simmer, covered, for about 15 to 20 minutes or until chicken is no longer pink inside.

3. Stir to combine and ladle chili into bowls.

Oven Variation

Proceed as directed in Stovetop Method through step 1. Cover and bake in preheated 400°F (200°C) oven for about 45 minutes or until chicken is no longer pink inside. Proceed with step 3.

Slow Cooker Variation

Place ingredients as directed in a minimum 4½-qt slow cooker. Cover and cook on High for about 1 hour or until chicken is no longer pink inside and thoroughly cooked. Proceed with Stovetop Method step 3.

Pressure Cooker Method

1. Spread chicken pieces in the bottom of pressure cooker. Scatter corn and beans over top of chicken; pour tomatoes evenly over. Sprinkle with ranch seasoning and chili powder. Place cream cheese on top.

2. Lock the pressure lid into place. Heat the pot over high heat and bring pressure to High. Cook for 6 minutes, adjusting heat to maintain pressure as necessary. Remove from heat and let the pressure release naturally.

3. Uncover pot. Stir to combine and ladle chili into bowls.

Bread Pairing

Corn and Jalapeño Jack Waffles (page 72)

Easy Chicken Ranch Chili (page 252) and Corn and Jalapeño Jack Waffles (page 72)

Easy Beef Chili

This is another easy but delicious recipe from my daughter Abby, who lives in Virginia. As a youth pastor's wife and mother of five, she likes to have an easy cold weather meal to serve her busy family. To satisfy the heat tolerance of some of her younger ones, she goes light on the chili powder and doesn't use the pepper sauce.

MAKES 4 TO 5 SERVINGS

- Large pot

Tips

Instead of buying canned beans, you can easily cook dried beans in the pressure cooker. See page 29 for instructions. For the can called for in the recipe, use 1½ cups (270 g) drained, rinsed cooked beans. For this recipe, you'll need to soak and cook about ⅔ cup (133 g) dried beans.

Chili has tons of flavor and flavor options with so many versions to satisfy every taste, with multiple meat and bean options to choose from. And of course, the kick! You can spice it up for the heat lovers or tone it down to be more family friendly. The choice is yours.

1 lb	lean ground beef	454 g
1	large onion, chopped	1
2	cloves garlic, minced	2
2 to 3 tbsp	chili powder	36 to 54 g
2	stalks celery, diced	2
1	can (28 oz / 796 g) tomatoes	1
2 tsp	salt	12 g
1 tsp	granulated cane sugar	3 g
1 tsp	Worcestershire sauce	5 g
½ tsp	hot pepper sauce, optional	2 g
1	can (14 to 15 oz / 398 to 425 g) red kidney beans, drained and rinsed	1

TOPPINGS, OPTIONAL

Sour cream

Shredded Cheddar, mozzarella or Monterey Jack cheese

Stovetop Method

1. In a large pot, cook ground beef and onions over medium heat, stirring and breaking up meat into chunks, until meat is browned and onions are softened. Add garlic and chili powder to taste; cook, stirring, for 1 minute, until fragrant. Add celery, tomatoes, salt, sugar, Worcestershire sauce and hot pepper sauce to taste (if using). Bring to a boil, stirring occasionally.

2. Cover, reduce heat to low and simmer, stirring occasionally, for about 1 hour, until slightly thickened. Stir in beans. Simmer, uncovered, stirring occasionally, for about 15 minutes, until heated through.

3. Ladle chili into bowls and serve topped with sour cream and cheese, if desired.

Bread Pairing

Cheddar Chili Bread Sticks (page 40)

Sue's Chuckwagon Beef Stew

This stew derives its name from the days of wagon trains, when nothing was wasted, not even leftover morning coffee. Brewed coffee adds a rich depth of flavor to beef dishes such as pot roast and beef stew. Use brewed or instant, regular or decaf coffee, as long as it's not flavored (and no cream and sugar, of course). And what could be better than a Butter Swim Biscuit to dip in this rich broth!

MAKES 6 TO 8 SERVINGS

- Large pot or minimum 6-qt (6 L) pressure cooker

Tips

You can use ½ cup (72 g) freshly milled hard wheat flour in place of the soft wheat in this recipe.

I learned the secret of adding a cup of black, unflavored coffee to my pot roast or beef stew from my mother-in-law when I was first married. As a non-coffee drinker, I was skeptical at first, but it adds such a rich flavor to the broth, I never make it any other way.

3 lbs	beef stew meat, cut into 1-inch (2.5 cm) chunks	1.36 kg
½ cup	freshly milled soft wheat flour (see Tip, left)	63 g
	Salt and freshly ground black pepper	
1 to 2 tbsp	olive oil (approx.)	14 to 28 g
1 cup	black brewed coffee (or prepared instant)	236 g
4 cups	beef stock or broth	944 mL
3 lbs	potatoes, cut into chunks	1.36 kg
1	sweet onion, coarsely chopped	1
½ lb	baby carrots, cut in half (or 3 to 4 medium carrots, cut into chunks)	227 g
1 tbsp	dried Italian seasoning	3 g

Stovetop Method

1. In a large bowl, toss stew meat with flour, 1 tsp (6 g) salt and pepper to taste.

2. In a large pot, heat 1 tbsp (14 g) of the oil over high heat. Add flour-coated beef, in batches, and cook, stirring, for about 4 minutes, until brown on all sides. Transfer to a bowl. Add more oil and adjust heat between batches, as necessary. Return beef and accumulated juices to pot. Sprinkle in any remaining flour mixture.

3. Gradually stir in coffee and stock; bring to a simmer, scraping up brown bits from bottom of the pot. Stir in potatoes, onion, carrots and Italian seasoning; return to a simmer, stirring occasionally.

4. Cover, reduce heat to low and simmer, stirring occasionally, for 1 to 2 hours or until beef and vegetables are tender and stew is thickened.

5. Uncover pot. Season with salt and pepper to taste. Ladle stew into bowls.

Pressure Cooker Method

1. In a large bowl, toss stew meat with flour, 1 tsp (6 g) salt and pepper to taste.

2. In a pressure cooker, heat 1 tbsp (14 g) of the oil over high heat. Add flour-coated beef, in batches, and cook, stirring, for about 4 minutes, until brown on all sides. Transfer to a bowl. Add more oil and adjust heat between batches, as necessary. Return beef and accumulated juices to pot. Sprinkle in any remaining flour mixture.

3. Gradually stir in coffee and stock; bring to a simmer, scraping up brown bits from bottom of the pot. Stir in potatoes, onion, carrots and Italian seasoning.

4. Lock the pressure lid into place. Heat the pot over high heat and bring pressure to High. Cook for 20 minutes, adjusting heat to maintain pressure as necessary. Remove from heat and let the pressure release naturally. The beef and vegetables should be tender. If not, return to pressure and cook in 2-minute increments until done.

5. Uncover pot. Season with salt and pepper to taste. Ladle stew into bowls.

Bread Pairing

Butter Swim Biscuits (page 80)

Sue's Chuckwagon Beef Stew (page 258)
and Butter Swim Biscuits (page 80)

Black-Eyed Pea and Beef Bratwurst Stew
with Cheesy Drop Biscuit Dumplings

When I was growing up in the southeastern United States, black-eyed peas were a mealtime staple. This flavorful stew is a favorite way to enjoy them. You do need to soak them before adding to the stew, so plan accordingly. Bratwurst adds a smokey flavor and cheesy dumplings soak up all the flavorful goodness as they simmer.

MAKE 6 TO 8 SERVINGS

- Large Dutch oven (see Tip, below) or minimum 6-qt (6 L) pressure cooker

Tips

It is best to use a more open pot such as a Dutch oven and a larger pressure cooker if you have one as opposed to a narrow stock pot, to have more surface room to drop in the dumplings.

To check the dumplings for doneness, using a slotted spoon, remove one dumpling from the stew and cut in half to check that the inside is no longer wet.

2 tbsp	olive oil	28 g
1 lb	smoked beef Bratwurst or other smoked sausage, sliced in rounds or half-moons	454 g
2 tbsp	unsalted butter	28 g
4	cloves garlic, minced	4
3	stalks celery, diced	3
1	large onion, chopped	1
1	jalapeño pepper, seeded and finely diced	1
1 tbsp	salt (approx.)	18 g
1 tsp	freshly ground black pepper (approx.)	2 g
8 cups	chicken stock or broth	1.89 L
1	can (14 to 15 oz / 398 to 425 g) diced tomatoes	1
½ lb	dried black-eyed peas, soaked and drained (see page 29)	227 g

CHEESY DROP BISCUIT DUMPLINGS

1¼ cups	freshly milled soft wheat flour	156 g
1½ tsp	baking powder	7 g
½ tsp	salt or garlic salt	3 g
½ cup	shredded Cheddar cheese	56 g
1 cup	buttermilk	240 g

Stovetop Method

1. In a large Dutch oven, heat oil over medium-high heat. Add sausage and cook, stirring occasionally, until browned. Using a slotted spoon, transfer sausage to a plate; set aside.

2. Return pot with oil to medium heat. Add butter, garlic, celery, onion and jalapeño; cook, stirring frequently, for about 5 minutes or until softened. Stir in the salt, pepper, stock and tomatoes. Stir in black-eyed peas and reserved sausage. Bring to a boil, stirring occasionally.

3. Cover, reduce heat to medium-low and boil gently, stirring occasionally, for about 45 minutes or until the peas are tender.

4. Cheesy Drop Biscuit Dumplings: In a medium bowl, whisk together flour, baking powder and salt. Add cheese and toss lightly to coat in flour. Pour in the buttermilk all at once and stir with a fork just until ingredients are combined. The batter will appear very loose. Let it stand for 1 to 2 minutes to thicken.

5. Reduce heat to low so that the stew is lightly simmering. Season with more salt and pepper to taste, if desired. Using a tablespoon or a small cookie scoop, drop spoonfuls of dumpling batter into the simmering soup, spacing them apart.

6. Cover the pot, leaving lid ajar, and simmer for about 15 to 20 minutes or until dumplings are cooked through (see Tip, opposite left). Remove from heat and let stand for a few minutes to let the dumplings "rest" before serving.

7. Ladle stew and dumplings into bowls.

Pressure Cooker Method

1. In a pressure cooker, heat oil over medium high heat. Add sausage and cook, stirring occasionally, until browned. Using a slotted spoon, transfer sausage to a plate; set aside.

2. Return pot with oil to medium heat. Add butter, garlic, celery, onion and jalapeño; cook, stirring frequently, for about 5 minutes or until softened. Stir in the salt, pepper, stock and tomatoes. Stir in black-eyed peas and reserved sausage. Bring to a boil, stirring occasionally.

3. Lock the pressure lid into place. Heat the pot over high heat and bring pressure to High. Cook for 10 minutes, adjusting heat to maintain pressure as necessary. Remove from heat and let the pressure release naturally. The peas should be tender. If not, return to pressure and cook in 2-minute increments until done.

4. Cheesy Drop Biscuit Dumplings: In a medium bowl, whisk together flour, baking powder and salt. Add cheese and toss lightly to coat in flour. Pour in the buttermilk all at once and stir with a fork just until ingredients are combined. The batter will appear very loose. Let it stand for 1 to 2 minutes to thicken.

5. Uncover the pot. Reduce heat to low so that the stew is lightly simmering. Season with more salt and pepper to taste, if desired. Using a tablespoon or a small cookie scoop, drop spoonfuls of dumpling batter into the simmering soup, spacing them apart.

6. Cover the pot, leaving lid ajar, and simmer for about 15 to 20 minutes or until dumplings are cooked through (see Tip, opposite left). Remove from heat and let stand for a few minutes to let the dumplings "rest" before serving.

7. Ladle stew and dumplings into bowls.

Black-Eyed Pea and Beef Bratwurst Stew with Cheesy Drop Biscuit Dumplings (page 262)

Brunswick Stew

In the state of Georgia, Brunswick Stew has long been a staple side dish, especially with any type of BBQ. But it also makes a delicious, hearty stew that can hold its own as a main dish on a cold day. There are many variations of this stew, each creator adding their own twists for the meat, but I have opted for a whole chicken. Some add lima beans, but ours only used corn. Feel free to make this basic recipe your own.

MAKES 6 TO 8 SERVINGS

- Large pot or minimum 6-qt (6 L) pressure cooker

1	whole chicken (2 to 3 lbs / 908 g to 1.36 kg)	1
4 to 6 cups	cold water	944 mL to 1.42 L
	Salt	
1	can (28 oz / 796 g) crushed tomatoes (see Tip, left)	1
2 cups	whole kernel corn	270 g
1 cup	prepared barbecue sauce	240 g
1 tbsp	Worcestershire sauce	15 g
	Freshly ground black pepper	

Tips

Use the extra stock immediately or place in a bowl or pot set in a sink full of ice water to rapidly cool, refreshing ice as necessary, until stock is cold. Skim off fat and discard, if desired. Transfer stock to jars or airtight containers and refrigerate for up to 3 days or freeze for up to 6 months.

In place of the crushed tomatoes, you can use canned diced or whole tomatoes. As you add tomatoes to the pot, crush them with your hands to break them into smaller pieces.

Stovetop Method

1. Place chicken breast-side down in a large pot. Add 4 cups (944 mL) water and heat on high. Add 1 tbsp (18 g) salt. Add more water to cover, if necessary. Bring to a boil.

2. Cover, reduce heat to low and simmer for about 45 minutes until chicken is tender and beginning to pull away from the bone.

3. Using tongs, transfer chicken from pot to a large bowl. Let chicken cool enough to handle. Measure 2 cups (472 g) stock for the stew; reserve remaining stock for another use (see Tip, opposite left). Remove skin and meat from bones; discard skin and bones. Finely shred meat and return to the pot with the measured stock.

4. Stir in tomatoes, corn, barbecue sauce and Worcestershire sauce. Bring to a simmer over medium heat. Reduce heat and simmer, stirring occasionally, for 15 to 20 minutes until flavors are blended and stew is heated through, being careful that it does not scorch.

5. Season to taste with salt and pepper. Ladle into bowls.

Pressure Cooker Method

1. Place chicken breast-side down in a pressure cooker. Add 4 cups (944 mL) cold water and heat on high. Add 1 tbsp (18 g) salt. Add more water to cover if necessary, ensuring you don't exceed maximum fill line in pressure cooker.

2. Lock the pressure lid into place. Heat the pot over high heat and bring pressure to High. Cook for 15 minutes, adjusting heat to maintain pressure as necessary. Remove from heat and let pressure release naturally. The chicken should be tender and beginning to pull away from the bone. If not, return to pressure and continue to cook in 2-minute increments until chicken is tender.

3. Uncover pot. Using tongs, transfer chicken from pot to a large bowl. Let chicken cool enough to handle. Measure 2 cups (472 g) stock for the stew; reserve remaining stock for another use (see Tip, opposite left). Remove skin and meat from bones; discard skin and bones. Finely shred meat and return to the pot with the measured stock.

4. Stir in tomatoes, corn, barbecue sauce and Worcestershire sauce. Bring to a simmer over medium heat. Reduce heat and simmer, stirring occasionally, for 15 to 20 minutes until flavors are blended and stew is heated through, being careful that it does not scorch.

5. Season to taste with salt and pepper. Ladle into bowls.

Bread Pairing

Parmesan Pull-Apart Rolls (page 43)

Brunswick Stew (page 266) and Parmesan Pull-Apart Rolls (page 43)

Ezekiel Stew

In 1999, as the year 2000 approached, there was widespread concern about how the change in numbering would affect our computer technology–based systems, particularly our power grid. People were expecting the worst from Y2K. Our Ezekiel Mixture of grains and beans, containing wheat, spelt, barley, millet, lentil, kidney beans, Great Northern beans and pinto beans, became a popular food storage item. To answer concerns about how to use whole grains and beans without power or a grain mill, I developed this delicious stew from this mixture that can even be cooked over a fire, without electricity, if needed.

10 TO 12 SERVINGS (SEE TIP, BELOW)

- Large pot or minimum 6-qt (6 L) pressure cooker

Tips

The metric weights have been calculated as precise conversions from imperial volumes. For ease, you can round the quantities up or down slightly in this stew and still get good results.

If you don't have all three of the kidney, pinto and Great Northern beans, you can use 3 tbsp (39 g) of any variety of dried beans (just one variety or a mixture).

This recipe is easy to double to make enough for a crowd. You'll need a very large pot or an 8-qt (8 L) pressure cooker for a double batch.

You can vary the quantity of potatoes, garlic and cumin you use based on your taste and what you have on hand.

$1\frac{1}{4}$ cups	hard red wheat berries	275 g
$\frac{3}{4}$ cup	spelt or rye berries	150 g
$\frac{1}{4}$ cup	hulled barley	45 g
2 tbsp	millet	27 g
2 tbsp	dried green or brown lentils	28 g
1 tbsp	dried red or white kidney beans	13 g
1 tbsp	dried pinto beans	13 g
1 tbsp	dried Great Northern beans	13 g
1 or 2	potatoes, cubed	1 or 2
1	onion, diced	1
1 or 2	cloves garlic, minced	1 or 2
1 to $1\frac{1}{2}$ tbsp	ground cumin	6 to 9 g
	Salt and freshly ground black pepper	
10 cups	chicken, beef or vegetable stock or broth	2.36 L

Stovetop Method

1. In a large pot, combine wheat berries, spelt berries, barley, millet, lentils, kidney beans, pinto beans, Great Northern beans, potatoes, onion, garlic, cumin, 1½ tsp (9 g) salt, ½ tsp (1 g) pepper and stock. Bring to a boil over high heat.

2. Cover, reduce heat to low and simmer, stirring occasionally and more often near the end of cooking, for about 2 to 3 hours until grains are soft and tender.

3. Uncover pot. Stir and season with more salt and pepper, if desired.

Pressure Cooker Method

1. In a pressure cooker combine wheat berries, spelt berries, barley, millet, lentils, kidney beans, pinto beans, Great Northern beans, potatoes, onion, garlic, cumin, 1½ tsp (9 g) salt, ½ tsp (1 g) pepper and stock. Bring to a boil over high heat; stir.

2. Lock the pressure lid into place. Heat the pot over high heat and bring pressure to High. Cook for 45 minutes, adjusting heat to maintain pressure as necessary. Remove from heat and let pressure release naturally.

3. Uncover pot. Stir and season with more salt and pepper, if desired.

Bread Pairing

Sun-Dried Tomato, Basil and Garlic Filled Bread (page 38)

Ezekiel Stew (page 270) and
Sun-Dried Tomato, Basil and Garlic Filled Bread (page 38)

Vegetable and Lentil Stew

This meatless, all-vegetable stew is full of flavor. It is easy to put together, with hands-on time less than 20 minutes. With a pressure cooker, it can be ready to serve in 30 minutes; stovetop cooking takes about an hour. Sit back and relax while it simmers or use the time to make drop biscuits or cornbread to go with it.

MAKES 8 SERVINGS

- Large pot or minimum 6-qt (6 L) pressure cooker

Tips

I like to use fire-roasted tomatoes in this stew to boost the flavor, although plain diced tomatoes work, too.

I prefer slender zucchini for cooking in stews like this one as they have less seeds.

¼ cup	olive oil	57 g
4	large carrots, sliced	4
2	onions, chopped	2
2 tbsp	chopped fresh parsley	6 g
1½ tsp	salt	9 g
1½ tsp	freshly ground black pepper	3 g
1 tsp	ground cumin	2 g
½ tsp	ground ginger	1 g
½ tsp	dried tarragon	0.5 g
1 lb	dried green or brown lentils, rinsed	454 g
8 cups	vegetable stock or broth	1.89 L
1	can (28 oz / 796 g) diced tomatoes (see Tip, left)	1
5 oz	fresh spinach, trimmed, leaves torn in half	142 g
3	medium zucchini (see Tip, left), chopped	3
	Additional chopped fresh parsley, optional	

Stovetop Method

1. In a large pot, heat oil over medium heat. Add carrots, onions, parsley, salt, pepper, cumin, ginger and tarragon; cook, stirring, for about 5 minutes or until onions are softened and spices are fragrant. Stir in lentils, stock and tomatoes. Bring to a boil over high heat.

2. Cover, reduce heat to low and simmer, stirring occasionally, for about 45 minutes or until lentils are the desired tenderness.

3. Stir in spinach and zucchini. Simmer, uncovered, stirring occasionally, for about 10 to 12 minutes or until zucchini is tender.

4. Ladle into bowls and sprinkle with additional parsley, if desired.

Pressure Cooker Method

1. In a pressure cooker, heat oil over medium heat. Add carrots, onions, parsley, salt, pepper, cumin, ginger and tarragon; cook, stirring, for about 5 minutes or until onions are softened and spices are fragrant. Stir in lentils, stock and tomatoes.

2. Lock the pressure lid into place. Heat the pot over high heat and bring pressure to High. Cook for 8 minutes, adjusting heat to maintain pressure as necessary. Remove from heat and let pressure release naturally or quick-release the pressure.

3. Uncover pot and return to low heat. Stir in spinach and zucchini. Simmer, uncovered, for about 10 to 12 minutes or until zucchini is tender.

4. Ladle into bowls and sprinkle with additional parsley, if desired.

Bread Pairing

Easy Drop Biscuits (page 76) or
Dill and Feta Cheese Drop Biscuits (page 79)

Vegetable and Lentil Stew (page 274) and
Easy Drop Biscuits (page 76)

Hungarian Mushroom Stew

There are many versions of this traditional Hungarian soup or stew, but what makes it authentic is the use of paprika. You will find it as a main spice in most Hungarian dishes, including the famous Hungarian Goulash. Some may call this a soup, but the thick broth makes me want to put it in the stew category. It's rich, creamy and warming, with a diverse flavor profile that makes it an interesting taste experience and by far one of my favorites.

MAKES ABOUT 6 SERVINGS

- Medium pot

Tips

Tamari is a Japanese fermented soy sauce using only 100 percent soybeans and no wheat. It is usually less salty than traditional Chinese soy sauce and has a richer flavor and darker color. It is available in the international ingredient section of most food stores. I prefer to use organic tamari because it is made with identity preserved soybeans and I choose to avoid consuming foods with GMOs.

The fresh dill for serving may seem optional but the fresh herb really brings out the other flavors of this stew.

¼ cup	unsalted butter	57 g
1	large onion, chopped	1
1 lb	baby bella (cremini) mushrooms, sliced	454 g
1 tbsp	Hungarian sweet or hot paprika (see box, opposite right)	6 g
2 cups	chicken stock or broth	472 g
1 tbsp	tamari sauce	15 g
1 tsp	dried dillweed	1 g
3 tbsp	freshly milled soft wheat flour	24 g
1 cup	whole milk	240 g
½ cup	sour cream	123 g
¼ cup	fresh parsley, chopped	12 g
1 tbsp	fresh lemon juice	15 g
1 tsp	salt	6 g
¼ tsp	ground black pepper	0.5 g
	Fresh dill fronds	

Stovetop Method

1. In medium pot, melt butter over medium heat. Add onion and cook, stirring, for about 5 minutes or until softened. Add mushrooms and cook, stirring, for about 5 minutes or until tender. Add paprika and cook, stirring, for about 1 minute, until fragrant.

2. Stir in stock, tamari and dillweed. Bring to a boil over high heat. Cover, reduce heat to low and simmer for 15 minutes.

3. Meanwhile, in a small bowl, whisk flour into milk. Gradually pour milk mixture into the stew, while whisking. Cover and simmer for 15 minutes, stirring occasionally, until thickened and flavors are blended.

4. Uncover pot. Stir in sour cream, parsley, lemon juice, salt and pepper. Cover and simmer for 1 to 2 minutes or until heated through.

5. Ladle stew into bowls and top with dill fronds.

HUNGARIAN PAPRIKA

Paprika is a spice made from the dried and ground pods of several different varieties of the Capsicum annum pepper. In Hungary, paprika is an everyday kitchen spice and creates the distinctive flavor of most soups, stews and other main dishes.

There are several varieties of Hungarian paprika, from sweet to hot. But no matter which variety and heat level you use, to bring out the best flavor, the paprika must be added to the hot fat and cooked briefly before the other ingredients are added.

Bread Pairing

Dark Molasses Sweet Bread with Homemade Garlic Honey Butter (pages 56 and 59)

Hungarian Mushroom Stew (page 278) and Dark Molasses Sweet Bread with Homemade Garlic Honey Butter (pages 56 and 59)

INDEX

A

B

C

M

N

O

P

Q

R

S

T

V

W

Y

Z

Library and Archives Canada Cataloguing in Publication
Title: Sue Becker's homemade bread, soups & stews cookbook : family recipes made with home-ground flour and wholesome ingredients.
Other titles: Homemade bread, soups and stews cookbook
Names: Becker, Sue, 1955- author
Description: Includes index.
Identifiers: Canadiana 20260184438 | ISBN 9780778807407 (softcover)
Subjects: LCSH: Soups. | LCSH: Bread. | LCSH: Stews. | LCGFT: Cookbooks.
Classification: LCC TX757 .B37 2026 | DDC 641.81/3—dc23